MOUNT HOPE

ROCHESTER, NEW YORK

America's First Municipal Victorian Cemetery

PHOTOGRAPHS BY FRANK A. GILLESPIE
TEXT BY RICHARD O. REISEM

Published by the Landmark Society of Western New York
Rochester, New York 14608-2204

First published 1994
Second Printing 1995
Third Printing 1999

Library of Congress Catalog Card Number: 94-65976
ISBN: 0-9641706-3-9

Come near my friends and cast an eye;
Then go your way, prepare to die.
Learn here your doom, and know you must
One day like me be turned to dust.

Inscription on the tombstone of
William Norris, died April 7, 1859, aged 30 years.
Range 1, Lot 125, Mount Hope Cemetery.

Printed in the United States of America
on 100# Somerset Gloss Text by
Printing Methods, Inc., Rochester, New York 14606

CONTENTS

A BRIEF HISTORY OF MOUNT HOPE

Mount Hope Cemetery in Rochester, New York, has the distinction of being the first municipal Victorian cemetery in America. It is a distinction that did not come about by accident. Mount Hope, established in 1838, is a 196-acre, landscaped burial ground set in a geological formation of dramatic eskers and kettles left by glaciers. The setting and the urgent needs of the city resulted in this unique cemetery.

THE TRANSFORMATION OF CEMETERIES.

Such a cemetery as Mount Hope would have been inconceivable in the 1000 years of western civilization before the 19th century. The custom had been to bury the dead inside parish churches, or if not inside, at least in close proximity in adjacent churchyards. Sometimes there were mass graves that were later ritualistically exhumed and the piles of skulls and bones assembled in macabre displays in the arcades of funerary chapels. These burials and exhumations were necessary to make more room, but they often occurred in such rapid succession that the dead became a serious menace to the living by fostering disease through unresolved decay. The conditions of London cemeteries in the early 1800s were so appalling that a plan to bury people, however neatly, 14 bodies deep was considered a proposal for improvement.

Simultaneously with the overcrowding of gravesites, there was a sharp growth in population that increased the pressure for change. But it was not just a matter of sanitation. Western civilization underwent a dramatic change in its attitudes toward death. In a revolution of attitudes, medieval Christian beliefs were replaced by romantic concepts in which there was a celebration of human death and nature. "Dust to dust" was tied to the rebirth of nature's beauty.

The result was the establishment of rural, garden cemeteries. Here, away from city centers, there was ample space, elimination of hygienic problems, and the newly welcomed association of nature with divinity. Since this burial reformation took place during the reign of Queen Victoria, these new rural, landscaped burial grounds became known as Victorian cemeteries.

PERE LACHAISE.

The first major rural, garden cemetery wasn't in England at all, but rather in France, outside of Paris. It is the Cemetery of Pere Lachaise, and it is undoubtedly the most famous landscaped, rural cemetery in the western world. Pere Lachaise opened in 1804, and the trend it established only later spread to England and America.

The first American example that is indebted to Pere Lachaise is Mount Auburn, a private cemetery established in 1831 outside of Boston. Kensal Green was established outside London in 1832. It is also a private cemetery. So when Rochester dedicated Mount Hope in 1838, it became the first Victorian cemetery to be planned, developed, and maintained by a municipality.

BOOMTOWN ROCHESTER.

In the 1830s Rochester rather quickly developed an urgent need for expanded burial space. The city was, after all, America's first boomtown, and its bulging population was quickly outgrowing available facilities. The towns around Rochester are generally older than the city itself. Early pioneers considered the area now occupied by Rochester to be uninhabitable. There were rattlesnakes, bears, and wolves. There were swamps, mosquitoes, and killing fevers. But, and this was the turning point, there were several waterfalls, including one that was 96-feet high. The power available from these dramatic drops in the Genesee River could not be overlooked. So, finally, in 1812, a village was formed along the river and its falls. Three factors created a boomtown out of this modest village: The surrounding countryside was abundantly fertile and suited to raising wheat; the Genesee Falls provided ample waterpower to mill flour from the wheat, and the construction of the Erie Canal, which opened in 1823, provided inexpensive transportation to ship flour to markets in eastern U.S. and Europe. With the completion of the canal, Rochester was on its way to becoming the Flour Capital of the World.

PIONEER BURIALS.

The earliest settlers in Rochesterville, as it was first known, laid their dead in the woods near the village. In fact, the first known burial of a white man here was in a grave dug near the river's edge just below High Falls. As the village grew, common burying grounds were established. The first such graveyard was created somewhat arbitrarily one day during the construction of the Johnson-Seymour Millrace. Stone was being removed and dumped over the east bank of the Genesee River. One of the men got his heavily loaded wagon too close to the bank, and he, the wagon, and his team of horses all plunged over the edge. The man was instantly killed, and before sunset, a group of his fellow workers recovered his body, built a coffin, and carried the body out to a spot in the woods roughly where East Avenue and Gibbs Street intersect today. It became a common village burial ground for a number of years even though the owner of the land, Enos Stone, never deeded the land to the village.

In 1820, two acres of a farm near what is now Monroe Avenue and Alexander Street were bought by the village for $100 to be used as a burying ground. All the burials from the East Avenue/Gibbs Street site were transferred to a common pit in the new grounds. The first lease for a lot in the Monroe Avenue graveyard was sold in 1820 for a period of 500 years, which would come up in the year 2320. But it turned out that the bodies buried there rested in peace only until 1872 when the city decided to build a school on the site. So, most of the burials, including the contents of the common pit, were moved to Mount Hope.

It was a similar story on the west side of the river. Col. Nathaniel Rochester, founder of the city, and his two partners, Col. William Fitzhugh and Major Charles Carroll, gave the village one-half acre for burial purposes at our present Plymouth Avenue and Spring Street. In just a few years, the uncomplaining tenants of that one-half acre were transferred to a 3 1/2-acre Buffalo Street graveyard. The first burial at Buffalo Street was the young and beautiful wife of Dr. Orrin Gibbs. Her lonely grave was guarded nightly for weeks against the wolves. Then, in 1851, the city acquired that Buffalo Street land for a hospital, so a transfer of graves was made to Mount Hope.

Rochester Catholics preferred their own burial grounds. There was St. Joseph on Lyell Avenue, Sts. Peter and Paul on Maple Street, and St. Boniface on South Clinton Avenue. The Catholics also maintained a small burying ground on Pinnacle Hill for 33 years. But the light, sandy soil there was mined for building purposes, so the Catholics transferred their burials to Holy Sepulchre Cemetery when it was established in 1871.

Rochester's oldest burying ground was started in the 1790s at King's Landing on Eastman Avenue and the river gorge. The cemetery is still there although the exact gravesites have been lost. Another early burying ground is Charlotte Cemetery near the mouth of the Genesee River. It is famous for holding the remains of Sam Patch, a daredevil who leaped to his death over High Falls on Friday, November 13, 1829, and whose body was found the next spring in the Genesee River near where he is now buried. A third small graveyard was established in 1812 on what is now Congress Avenue near the southern end of Genesee Street. In those days, the Genesee River formed rapids at this point, and so the spot became known as the Rapids burying ground. King's Landing, Charlotte, and Rapids cemeteries are the only early burial grounds in the city of Rochester to survive to this day.

THE CHOLERA EPIDEMIC.

In 1822, the year before the Erie Canal was completed, the population of Rochester was 2,700, already swollen from the 300 of a decade before because of thriving mills and canal workers. A mere 4 years later, in 1826, the population had almost tripled to 7,670.

Rochester was not spared the cholera epidemics sweeping the country and Europe in the early part of the 19th century. In 1832, about 120 Rochesterians died of the disease. Burying them took all of the available lots in the Buffalo Street burying ground. The other small community graveyards and churchyards were similarly crowded. City fathers faced a three-pronged emergency: Overcrowding of an existing proliferation of tiny burying grounds; possible contamination of drinking water that came from wells near the graveyards, and urgent need for commercial and industrial development of the downtown land that was devoted to burials.

THE FIGHT FOR A SITE.

On August 24, 1836, Alderman David Scoville offered a resolution in Rochester Common Council "that a committee be formed to inquire into the expediency of purchasing Silas Andrus' lot on the east side of the river, or any other lot near the city, for a burial ground." With the adoption of that resolution and the appointment of a committee to pursue it came the controversy. Powerful and influential William A. Reynolds strongly favored the west bank of Irondequoit Bay, but the committee selected the Silas Andrus site. General Jacob Gould, not known for a restrained demeanor, condemned the choice as being "all up hill and down dale, and with a gully at the entrance at that."

"That committee deserve desecration," boomed General Gould. "Why, that ground isn't fit for pasturing rabbits." The cheery response Gould received was, "But we are not going to pasture rabbits."

Mrs. Joseph Strong decided to see this place for herself, and she drove out to the woods where the new cemetery was to be located. She had hoped it would be a place she could visit occasionally, but the deep, unbroken woods and the inaccessible hilltops and gullies would not even do for a picnic, she said, much less a cemetery. Others maintained the land was only suitable for hunting wild animals.

Then there was the issue of the land cost. Silas Andrus had purchased 53 and 86/100 acres in 1822 for $287. Now, in 1836, he wanted $100 an acre, or $5,386. The outcry against municipal wastefulness and folly was loud, but the committee was sure of its choice, and on December 27, 1836, the city acquired the nucleus of what would become Mount Hope Cemetery and acquired it at Mr. Andrus' price.

The site was one and a half miles from downtown, an amply safe distance from the wells that provided drinking water in the city. It was large enough in size to accommodate the needs even of a city with an exploding population. And it was rural, permitting communion with nature. Interestingly, General Jacob Gould was one of the first to purchase land and build a conspicuous family vault right in the west hillside of that gully entrance he so deplored.

WHAT THE CITY BOUGHT.

In a letter that he wrote some 50 years after Mount Hope Cemetery was established, one Rochester citizen described the scene before the city's purchase of the land. At the proposed entrance to the future cemetery, he said, "there was a low, swampy place in there filled in with a perfect mat of high alders, choke cherries, and high-bush huckleberries. People said that lights moved around there in the daytime, and in the night would start up and move off up into the hills, and that horrid sounds had been heard. We boys always ran like a streak through there, or if we had a horse, we put him through on double-quick until we rose on the hill going by Judge Warner's. Messrs. Ellwanger and Barry and Judge Warner may smile now when they look out on the beauties that they and kindred workers have spread all over this once haunted place. To think that in the recollection of any citizen, it was literally a howling wilderness -- so howling with wild beasts that at night, alone and unarmed, no individual dared venture along the road there, much less to penetrate the woods at the base of those hills, where in late years Mr. Hamilton, the old Scotch milkman, had smuggled in his little house and stable nearly out of sight of the road. But that was so, and I can remember when no common Indian, versed as he might be with the voices of the wild animals of the forests, could interpret the discordant sounds of beast and fowl and frog that were sprung upon the air there, any fall night. It was through this passage that George G. Sill of Old Lyme, Connecticut -- afterwards the first bookseller in Rochester -- had to be escorted in the night by Daniel Harris, because the road was so blind, and there were so many bears and wolves in that neighborhood."

GEOLOGY OF MOUNT HOPE.

About 12,000 to 14,000 years ago, Mount Hope was covered with ice one to two miles thick. As the glacier receded, cracks appeared in the ice, and these crevasses became rivers of water and gravel. When the miles-high ice sheet finally melted, these river beds were left as ridges created from all the rock and rubble that had been deposited by the flowing river. In geological terms, these ridges are called eskers. One such esker snakes its way through much of Mount Hope Cemetery. The Seneca Indians used it as a trail from the Bristol Hills south of Rochester to Lake Ontario on the city's northern border. For them, it provided a continuous high path through the moraine and visibility of the valleys around them. Today, this esker is a principal vehicular lane through the cemetery and is called Indian Trail Avenue.

Another geological feature of Mount Hope is what are called kettles. At the leading edge of the receding glacier, large blocks of ice would break off from the main glacier and float freely in the glacial lake. These icebergs would then become surrounded or covered by gravel and debris flowing off the ice sheet. When the icebergs melted and the glacial lake disappeared, there were deep conical holes left in the resulting landscape. Four large kettles were formed in Mount Hope Cemetery, one of which has remained filled with water and is called Sylvan Waters. Grave plots were later developed in likely spots on even some of these steepest inclines.

The sharp rise and fall of the land in Mount Hope Cemetery, while hardly ideal for farming, proved dramatic and picturesque for development as a park-garden-cemetery. The high points in Mount Hope Cemetery are at an elevation of 650 to 675 feet. The highest point in the city is Pinnacle Hill at 749 feet. For comparison, the Erie Canal carried water through the city at an elevation of 508 feet, and the street elevation downtown at Four Corners is 499 feet.

CIVILIZING THE WILDERNESS.

The city mayor, Elisha Johnson; three aldermen, Elias Pond, Joseph Strong, and Isaac Mack; and the city surveyor, Silas Cornell, constituted a committee to devise a plan for laying out the grounds of the new cemetery. They asked for the assistance of Major David Bates Douglass, a distinguished army officer and civil engineering professor, who laid out the grounds at Green-Wood Cemetery in Brooklyn, as well as cemeteries in Albany and Quebec. But there were serious differences of opinion between the committee and Major Douglass concerning the approach to be used. The committee wanted minimal disturbance of the trees and the dramatic undulations of the landscape, so finally it fell to Silas Cornell to design the cemetery layout. It was a fortunate decision for posterity. Cornell's rare skill as a landscape architect and his wise decisions on the placement of roads and features, as well as his judicious clearing of trees transformed the place from its primitive condition to one of the most beautiful and enchanting cemeteries in America.

NAMING THE CEMETERY.

Silas Cornell proposed naming the new cemetery "Mount Auburn" after the one he had seen and admired in Boston, but many Rochesterians thought that name gave a feeble impression. For many months, the cemetery remained nameless, and all transactions having to do with the preparatory work at the new burying ground had a deliberate blank where the name of the cemetery should have appeared. However, there was a laborer at the cemetery, William Wilson, who when he submitted his bills for services in 1838 persisted in using the phrase "for labor at Mount Hope." Gradually, without any formal adoption, the name, Mount Hope, just got accepted and has been applied ever since laborer Wilson's personal invoices proffered the appellation.

DEDICATION OF THE CEMETERY.

On October 3, 1838, Mount Hope Cemetery was dedicated. Burials had started before the dedication; the first interment was William Carter, who was buried on August 18, 1838. At the dedication ceremonies Dr. Whitehouse of St. Luke's Church read a consecration service; the choir of St. Luke's sang; a soprano delivered appropriate anthems, and the Rev. Pharcellus Church, pastor of the First Baptist Church, presented an inspired dedication address. The following comprises several excerpts from that address:

"At few points on the surface of the globe has nature been more liberal in its provisions for giving scope to these principles than in the neighborhood of our own city. Rural scenery, undulating surface, inviting features, both of beauty and sublimity, ponds that may be easily cleared and made to present a smooth and shining expanse as of molten silver, a dry and light soil, peculiarly favorable alike to the opening of graves and the preservation of them from the intrusion of water, and a location retired, and yet sufficiently contiguous to our city, are some of the advantages which conspire to make Mount Hope one of the most inviting cemeteries in the world.

"Good judges who have visited both, pronounce its scenery even more bold and picturesque than that of the celebrated Mount Auburn in the neighborhood of Boston. In the small improvements which have been made on these grounds, how many interesting features have been developed! As we slowly wind round the mount, gradually rising to its summit like life in its advancing stages, we meet abrupt declivities, deeply shaded valleys, natural arbors, towering heights, with their superincumbent weight of primeval forest, narrow ridges, on which you seem to poise between the deep descent on either hand, while your eye searches in vain for the bottom lands below.

"And when you stand on the summit itself, how enchanting is the prospect! The smooth current of the Genesee meandering round the base, and stealing its now obvious and now concealed way to the distant lake, like the passing of life through shade and sunshine to the ocean of eternity.

"Around you see, spread out in ample view, the rich fields of one of the richest countries in the world, sending their loaded harvests to the marts of trade and supplying the staff of life to millions of people. Before you lies the thronged city, with its spires and minarets pointing to heaven, while the clatter of machinery, or the deep-toned bell, or the voices of living multitudes, united to the roar of the neighboring cascades, all send up to heaven a voice as deafening and discordant as the cries of factious clans in the world's tumultuous theatre. Far off beyond the city, the broad blue Ontario skirts the undefined distance, as if to remind you of the boundless fields of existence which eternity will unfold, and to make you feel how few and meagre are the objects subjected to our present inspection compared with those in the distance which a future world will disclose.

"By the order and in behalf of our municipal board, I do now formally declare this wild retreat dedicated to the repose of the dead, henceforth and forever. In the highest sense in which a transfer can be made, Mount Hope by this act passes from the hand of the living to the hand of the dead. It is an inviolable and unending trust. Nevermore shall the dwellings or occupations of the living obtrude within these sacred precincts. Whatever is here transacted shall be done in furtherance of the ends of this our solemn dedication.

"Let this place henceforth be visited to revive the memory of departed friends and to anticipate the exalted scenes of eternity."

In Section H of the cemetery there is a headstone for Samuel Miller. The inscription on the stone reads, "Aged 4 yrs, 2 mos, died Oct. 3, 1838, at 2:30 p.m., the precise time when this cemetery was consecrated and his was the first burial in it after the consecration."

SHADE TREES FROM ELLWANGER & BARRY.

Across Mount Hope Avenue from the cemetery was the Ellwanger & Barry Nursery, started in 1840. At its height, the nursery occupied 650 acres and was the largest in the world. In 1847, Ellwanger & Barry presented a gift of 50 shade trees to Mount Hope Cemetery for the occasion of the cemetery's tenth anniversary. It was also a gesture designed to encourage the city to persist in its efforts to improve an already famous cemetery. These trees -- including European purple, fernleaf, and weeping beeches, as well as Nikko fir, Caucasian spruce, Norway maple, and variegated sycamore maple trees -- were strategically planted in the older section of the cemetery and have become over the last almost 150 years great specimen trees. These plantings complement the original forest which was only partially cut when the cemetery was prepared for burials. The largest and best trees were carefully saved during this preparatory work. The dominant species of that original forest were red, black, and white oaks. Some of these oaks are now well over 300 years old. The original forest also includes chestnuts, American beeches, red and sugar maples, basswoods, tuliptrees, and white ashes. Over the years many other species have been added making a particularly fascinating wooded melange.

ARCHITECTURE COMES TO MOUNT HOPE.

In 1859 a Gothic Revival entrance building incorporating an arched gateway was erected to replace the original Egyptian-style wooden structure. The stone Gothic building lasted 15 years. In 1874, Andrew Jackson Warner, one of upstate New York's most prominent architects, designed the present stone gate and gatehouse. A Gothic Revival chapel, designed by local architect, Henry Robinson Searle, was added in 1862. A charming Moorish Revival gazebo was built to house a water fountain. Then in 1875, a Florentine fountain of cast iron became the central focal point of a circular drive in the entrance area. Finally, to finish the architectural treatment at the original cemetery entrance, a crematory was added to the chapel. It has a smokestack that even the talented architect, J. Foster Warner, could not effectively disguise with Gothic Revival trappings.

THE CEMETERY EXPANDS.

Over the years bits and pieces were added to the cemetery's acreage -- 9.39 acres in 1839, another 9.02 in 1841, 4.22 more in 1861, and 13.16 acres in 1864. Then in 1865, from January 25 to November 3, in three separate purchases, 78.57 acres were acquired. With additional small land acquisitions since then, the cemetery today is 196 acres, where it will undoubtedly stay, hemmed in as it is by residential areas to the north and on the east side of Mount Hope Avenue and by the University of Rochester to the west and south.

Through these 196 acres, up and down the hills and twisting around the landscape, run 14 1/2 miles of roads. More than a few teenagers have learned their driving techniques from parents and friends on these winding roadways. At least one automobile has overturned on one of the downhill, blind, sharp curves. Jack McKinney and the author saw the accident happen in

1988. These lanes that used to be workouts for horses drawing carriages today challenge joggers, bicyclists, and cemetery tourgoers.

THE OBSERVATORY ON THE SUMMIT.

On his 100th birthday in 1915, John S. Wilson recalled, "Upon the summit of the hill at Mount Hope used to stand a tower containing an elevator, and for a piece of money they would elevate the visitor to the top of that tower for a view of Rochester and surrounding country. This was called 'The Fandango.'"

From the top of this wooden structure there were spectacular views of the Bristol mountains to the south and of the city, the river, and Lake Ontario to the north. Wilson's century-old memory may have failed him on this occasion. Many of us believe that it was necessary to climb stairs in that observatory, and climbing the stairs did not require the payment of "a piece of money." Wilson may have confused the elevator feature with the celebrated elevator in the Powers Building downtown, where for "a piece of money" you could indeed ride an elevator, the first one in Rochester, to the top of the tower, then the tallest building in town, for another magnificent view.

On April 16, 1871, the view to the north from the Fandango became even more spectacular than usual. It was a particularly bright and clear day, and the view was an eerie and yet glorious sight, for the Canadian shore appeared to be visible in great detail and positioned far closer than the actual distance of some 50 miles. People familiar with the landscape across Lake Ontario identified Canadian landmarks, lakes, and forests. The word of the awesome happening spread quickly around town, and thousands of Rochesterians climbed to the top of the Fandango during the course of the day to get a look. The incredible event was reported in Frank Leslie's Illustrated Newspaper and became known as "The Rochester Mirage." To this day the cause of the one-day phenomenon witnessed by thousands has been largely unexplained.

STREETCAR SERVICE TO MOUNT HOPE.

Streetcar service from downtown Rochester to Mount Hope commenced on July 9, 1863. The one-way trip was 1 1/2 miles for the horses pulling the streetcar. Years later, when one winter the horses got sick and were unable to climb Mount Hope Avenue, the young attorney/inventor George B. Selden offered to power the streetcar with his newly invented gasoline engine, and service was resumed.

THE IMPACT OF GEORGE D. STILLSON.

No single person probably did more to improve Mount Hope Cemetery than a civil engineer by the name of George D. Stillson who became superintendent of the cemetery in December, 1865, and served in that capacity until he died 16 years later in 1881. Stillson was the engineer of the famous Portage Bridge and could have had many other more lucrative positions, but he chose to serve Mount Hope. Besides his skills as an engineer, Stillson was an excellent landscape architect.

One of the conditions that Stillson felt marred the beauty of Mount Hope was a large marsh near the newly constructed chapel in the entrance area of the cemetery. His dramatic solution was a tunnel through the esker that carried Indian Trail Avenue on its crest. The concept of such an extended tunnel,which had to burrow more than 500 feet to emerge on the

Genesee River side of the hill, would still be greeted as a monumental engineering feat today. But Stillson did it. The entrance was located 8 feet south of the chapel, and the tunnel drained the marsh water to the Genesee River thereby opening a large area for lawns, trees, in-ground burial plots, and a number of mausoleums.

Throughout the cemetery, Stillson's consummate skill turned wasteland into attractive burial plots and public features of significance and beauty. But Stillson was more than an outstanding engineer and landscape architect to the cemetery. Under his leadership, better and more complete cemetery records were kept. And he was more than an expert accountant, too. His compassion to grieving families and kindness to the lowliest mourner were renowned. For those who feared their dead might be buried alive, he visited the open casket during the night in the chapel. In a resolution passed at the time of Stillson's death, the commissioners of the cemetery recognized "his fitness by nature and cultivation for the place he has so long honored that bears testimony to his good judgment, skill, and fidelity. Thousands have been comforted in their afflictions by his kind words, thousands have been assisted by his willing hands, and tens of thousands can bear testimony to the gentle sway he ever had in the last rites to the buried dead."

THE LOST MOUNT HOPE RECORDS.

The commissioners of Mount Hope Cemetery received a surprising letter from the sheriff of Lincoln County, Ontario, Canada, in March, 1884. In the letter the sheriff announced that records of Mount Hope Cemetery and our city treasurer's office had been found in St. Catharines. They turned out to be the cemetery records for 11 years, from 1846 to 1857, and the accounts of the cemetery endowment fund for the same period.

Everyone in Rochester thought that these records were destroyed in a fire at the Eagle Bank in 1857. Naturally, a vast amount of confusion concerning lots at Mount Hope was caused by the loss of the records. At the time of the bank fire, these records had been in the custody of John B. Robertson, the comptroller in charge of the cemetery endowment fund. Robertson alleged that the records were burned in the bank fire and shortly afterward, he left Rochester permanently and presumably to live in Canada.

But the records, of course, had not burned at all. Robertson had taken them to cover the fact that he had embezzled $40,000, a princely sum in 1857, from the cemetery endowment fund. Despite Robertson's theft, the cemetery's endowment fund has continued to grow to a current value of well over $3 million, the dividends and interest from which are used to help maintain Mount Hope today.

A UNIVERSAL CEMETERY.

Mount Hope Cemetery, being a municipal cemetery, is available to all -- paupers as well as millionaires, blacks and whites, all ethnic groups, all religious beliefs. There is no discrimination here. Many groups purchased sections of the cemetery for the use of their members. These groups include:

- Nine Jewish congregations,
- Civil War veterans,
- Spanish-American War veterans,
- World War I veterans,
- Sons and Daughters of the American Revolution,
- Rochester Fire Department,
- University of Rochester,

- Episcopal Church,
- Free and Accepted Masons,
- Independent Order of Odd Fellows,
- St. Andrews (Scottish) Society,
- The Megiddo Band,
- Rochester City Hospital,
- Rochester Orphan Asylum,
- Home for the Friendless,
- Western House of Refuge,
- Rochester German Benevolent Society,
- State Industrial School,
- United Sons of Rochester,
- Western New York Institute for Deaf Mutes,
- Society of Friends,
- Rochester Friendly Home, and
- St. John's Home.

THE FRIENDS OF MOUNT HOPE CEMETERY.

On the evening of December 6, 1979, Dr. Rowland Collins, then chairman of the English Department of the University of Rochester, called a meeting at his home to discuss the formation of a Friends of Mount Hope Cemetery organization that would be concerned with the preservation and public use of the cemetery. About 20 people, including several city administrators, gathered in Rowland and Sarah Collins' living room to endorse the idea enthusiastically. The organization began operating as a New York State not-for-profit corporation in 1980 with a mission: "To restore, preserve, and encourage the public use and enjoyment of the significant cultural resource that is Mount Hope Cemetery."

Although the cemetery is municipally owned and operated, much of the city's efforts are, of necessity, concerned with maintaining and operating an immense cemetery and crematory that are in daily use. The several hundred interested citizens who are members of The Friends of Mount Hope Cemetery believe that this unique cultural resource deserves restoration, beautification, education, and public use as a very interesting, historic, and exceptional park.

Today, the Friends staff of experienced tour guides give free guided walking tours on Sunday afternoons in the spring, summer, and fall. Special tours are also conducted for school children and interested organizations and groups throughout the year. Speakers present a slide/tape program to any interested group. The garden committee plants and maintains gardens throughout historic sections, and the Adopt-a-Plot program has individuals and groups maintaining many of the important gravesites. Other projects include restoration of the 1872 Moorish gazebo, the 1875 Florentine fountain, and the 1874 gatehouse; the repair and maintenance of historical burial sites; the addition of benches and amenities; and the staging of many special events. The organization has also put its energies and financial support behind the publication of this book.

MOUNT HOPE CEMETERY TODAY.

A concern of cemetery administrators is the eventual filling up of all available land which will eliminate the revenues obtained from the sale of plots and thus create a financial burden in order to continue cemetery maintenance. A number of innovative plans are under consideration to delay this eventuality as long as possible. One, already in practice, is the construction of lawn crypts that permit more than one burial in a single cemetery plot. This stacking of graves immediately multiplies the number of interments that can be handled on the remaining open land. Another plan that is likely to be adopted is the construction of columbaria, which have the capability of holding large numbers of cremation interments within a confined space.

Today, the cemetery remains rural, parklike, and uncrowded. The Victorian concept of death envisioned romantic landscaping and monuments -- great, specimen trees and granite, marble, bronze, and zinc monuments that reflected classical symbols from ancient Greek, Roman, and Egyptian civilizations or that represented highly personal ideas. To the Victorians, death was not the grim reaper it had been to early American settlers. Nor did death mean the utter finality of life that is the prevalent belief today. In Mount Hope, soaring Egyptian obelisks, miniature Greek temples, winged angels of mercy, draped Grecian urns and broken columns, granite tree trunks, stone and bronze dogs, and Christian saints are among the myriad funerary art forms that gloriously decorate the more than a third of a million graves. They stand as a testament of hope for life everlasting to a society that was different from ours and yet a society from which we all descend.

These monuments gain further effectiveness in the unusual terrain of Mount Hope, being the westward extension of the Pinnacle range of mountains that were left as a moraine when the last glacier receded 12,000 years ago. The resulting ridges and valleys, still heavily wooded, contain the thousands upon thousands of monuments at every visual level, reinforcing one another in a powerful chorus of man's hope and relationship to nature. If Mount Hope could be described in musical terms, it would definitely and definitively be Mahler. It is truly a breathtaking place to experience in person, and it is the wish of Frank Gillespie, whose evocative photographs appear on the following pages, and myself that these photographs elicit the exultant feeling and beauty of Mount Hope, as well as interpret its transcendental nature.

To the photographs we add an historical aspect, for Mount Hope tells fascinating stories of a boomtown American community that not only had an interesting local history but that had a significant impact -- with the lives of Susan B. Anthony, Frederick Douglass, and Hiram Sibley, just for example -- on our country and the world.

Mt. Hope Cemetery Map and Legend

1. 1874 gatehouse
2. 1862 chapel and original crematory
3. 1875 Florentine fountain
4. George Washington Aldrich, politician
5. 1872 gazebo
6. Hiram Sibley
7. Don Alonzo Watson
8. Roth monument
9. Bausch and Lomb
10. Susan B. Anthony
11. Margaret Woodbury Strong mausoleum
12. Henry R. Selden and George B. Selden
13. William Carter, first burial
14. Jonathan Child and Col. Nathaniel Rochester plots
15. Lewis Henry Morgan mausoleum
16. George Ellwanger
17. Frederick Douglass
18. Johnny Baker, foster son of Buffalo Bill
19. Sylvan Waters
20. Freeman Clarke monument
21. University of Rochester
22. Henry A. Ward monument
23. Elizabeth Hollister Frost, poet
24. Aaron Erickson monument
25. Gen. E. G. Marshall
26. Rochester Orphan Asylum
27. Nathan Stein mausoleum
28. Mayor Hiram Edgerton
29. John Snell, heroic engineer
30. Episcopal Church plot
31. Congregation Bene David
32. Congregation Beth Israel, Range 3
33. Congregation Beth El, Range 3
34. Megiddo Mission plot
35. Temple B'rith Kodesh
36. Congregation Beth El, Range 9
37. Masonic plot
38. Rochester Friendly Home
39. World War I plot
40. Spanish-American War
41. Civil War plot
42. St. John's Home for Aged
43. Odd Fellows, plot 2
44. Firemen's monument
45. D.A.R. monument
46. Odd Fellows, plot 1
47. Algernon Crapsey family plot, Adelaide Crapsey
48. Buffalo Bill's children
49. Hartwell Carver monument
50. Jacob Myers, inventor of the voting machine
51. 1912 chapel
52. Cemetery office/crematory
53. Seth Green, founder of fish hatcheries
54. Edward Mott Moore, M.D.
55. Myron Holley, canal builder
56. Henry O'Reilly, publisher
57. James Vick, nurseryman
58. James G. Cutler, architect
59. Edwin G. Strasenburg
60. Frank Gannett, publisher
61. Alexander Millener, Geo. Washington's drummer
62. Rabbi Phillip S. Bernstein
63. Lillian Wald, founder of public nursing

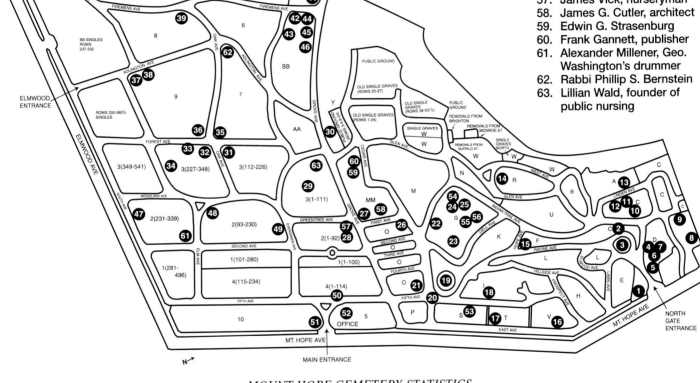

MOUNT HOPE CEMETERY STATISTICS.

- Size: 196 acres.
- Roads: 14 1/2 miles.
- Highest Elevation: 675 feet.
- Number of Geological Kettles: 4.
- Permanent Population: 350,000.
- Growth Rate: 500-600 burials annually.
- First Burial: William Carter, August 18, 1838.
- Dedication: October 3, 1838.
- First Burial After Dedication: Samuel Miller, who died at the precise time the cemetery was consecrated.
- Oldest Persons Buried: James Hard, 111 years, and Cynthia Fitzpatrick, 118 years.
- Number of Mausoleums: 74.
- Largest Mausoleum: Nathan Stein, sleeps 20.
- Tallest Monument: Firemen's Monument, 55'.

- Famous People (The Short List):
  Susan B. Anthony, women's rights;
  John Jacob Bausch, cofounder of Bausch & Lomb Company;
  Hartwell Carver, father of the transcontinental railroad;
  Frederick Douglass, abolitionist;
  Frank E. Gannett, publisher;
  Seth Green, inventor of fish hatcheries;
  Myron Holley, instigator and builder of the Erie Canal;
  Henry Lomb, cofounder of Bausch & Lomb;
  Lewis Henry Morgan, founder of the science of anthropology;
  Hiram Sibley, founder of Western Union and instigator of the purchase of Alaska.

THE A. J. WARNER / J. FOSTER WARNER TEAM.

The careers of father and son architects, Andrew Jackson Warner (1833-1910) and John Foster Warner (1859-1937), dominated the architectural scene in upstate New York from the late 1850s to the late 1920s. Both father and son were extremely prolific architects with an impressive list of highly distinguished office buildings, churches, schools, government buildings, banks, hotels, commercial buildings, hospitals, industrial buildings, and residences to their credit.

A number of their buildings are city landmarks and listed on New York State and Federal Registers of Historic Places. Some of their Rochester landmarks include:

- Bissell Residence (1854), A. J. Warner
- Powers Building (1865), A. J. Warner
- First Presbyterian Church (1871), A. J. Warner
- Rochester Free Academy (1872), A. J. Warner
- City Hall (1873), A. J. Warner
- St. Bernard's Seminary (1891), A. J. Warner
- George Eastman House (1905), J. Foster Warner
- Rochester Savings Bank (1926), J. Foster Warner

In Mount Hope Cemetery, these architects designed the following structures:

- Old Gatehouse and Gate (1874), A. J. Warner
- Old Crematory (1912), J. Foster Warner
- New Chapel (1912), J. Foster Warner

A. J. Warner is buried in Range 1, Lot 172, and J. Foster Warner is buried in Section C, Lot 107.

Previous pages: The Moorish-style gazebo, left-hand page, was erected in 1872 and recently restored by The Friends of Mount Hope Cemetery. The old cemetery gatehouse, right-hand page, was designed in High Victorian Gothic style by the famous Rochester architect, Andrew Jackson Warner, and built in 1874. It is now the office of The Friends of Mount Hope Cemetery.

At left, the new chapel, built in 1912, was designed by A. J. Warner's son, J. Foster Warner, who became as famous an architect as his father. Infrared film provides the ghostly appearance.

J. Foster Warner also designed the crematory addition, at right, that was attached in 1912 to the old 1862 Gothic Revival chapel. This was one of the earliest crematories built in the U.S., but even Warner's great design skill could not disguise the smokestack with Gothic details.

To the right of the chapel/crematory is the hillside vault, with Egyptian motifs including an obelisk on top, of General Jacob Gould.

GEORGE ELLWANGER.

Mount Hope Avenue owes its early development not just to the cemetery. George Ellwanger (1816-1906) and Patrick Barry started a nursery here in 1840, two years after the cemetery opened. Their nursery, which grew to 650 acres on the east side of Mount Hope Avenue opposite the cemetery, became the largest such operation in the world, and its international prominence was the principal reason that Rochester, when flour milling waned, changed to being "The Flower City."

The young George Ellwanger, who was born in Germany and studied horticulture and landscape gardening in Stuttgart, came to the U.S. in 1835 to open a nursery business in Tiffin, Ohio. The packet boat that carried him westward on the Erie Canal made a stopover in Rochester. It was a long-enough stay for young George to determine that Rochester had an ideal climate and particularly suitable soil for horticulture. But he went on to Tiffin anyway. He couldn't get Rochester out of his mind, however, and he came back to open his nursery here.

Ellwanger made frequent trips to Europe and brought back advanced horticultural methods and the most valuable trees and plants, many of which were unknown in this country. No other person in America introduced and propagated so many new varieties of trees and plants as did Ellwanger.

Among the countless innovations that he introduced are dwarf apple and pear trees and many celebrated varieties of fruits such as the Northern Spy apple. The great European beeches -- purple, fernleaf, and weeping -- that adorn Rochester and many other American cities are the result of Ellwanger's careful grafting and propagation.

Ellwanger commissioned the famous Italian sculptor, Nicola Cantalamessa-Papotti to create the marble representation of Saint John, depicted with an eagle by his left side, to be placed on his family monument. The inscription on the sculpture reads: "I heard a voice from heaven." Saint John is situated near Mount Hope Avenue not far from the land that was once the vast, incomparable Ellwanger & Barry Nursery.

St. John, hearing a voice from heaven, is poised to write the book of Revelation. He was sculpted in 1874 by the Italian artist, Nicola Cantalamessa-Papotti, for the George Ellwanger family monument located in Section V.

VOICE FROM HEAVEN

NICOLA CANTALAMESSA-PAPOTTI, ITALIAN SCULPTOR.

Two impressive marble sculptures in Mount Hope Cemetery were carved by Nicola Cantalamessa-Papotti (1833-1910). This talented Italian studied his art at an academy in Rome. His skills were quickly noticed. Ferdinand II, King of the Two Sicilies, commissioned a major work by the young sculptor. Then in 1856, when Papotti was just 23, Pope Pius IX commissioned him to sculpt a bas relief, St. Joseph's Dream, for the base of the column of the Immaculate Conception. These constituted a heady start to a long and distinguished career.

Papotti showed a lifesize work, Love's Mirror, at the Philadelphia Exposition in 1876. This work is now in the Memorial Art Gallery in Rochester.

Papotti received many private and public commissions for both religious and secular works, including cemetery monuments in Europe and the United States. He created a memorial for the assassinated President James A. Garfield.

Both George Ellwanger and his nursery partner, Patrick Barry, commissioned Papotti to create significant, lifesize sculptures for their family monuments -- Ellwanger's in Mount Hope Cemetery in 1874 and Barry's in Holy Sepulchre Cemetery in 1878.

The Weary Pilgrim is dated 1882. It depicts a pilgrim in the Crusades, with his symbolic scallop shell on his cloak, resting on his journey to the Holy Land.

Papotti's work is particularly appropriate for Mount Hope Cemetery. Both Saint John and the Weary Pilgrim capture the romantic feeling of the Victorian era. The imposing pedestals provided for both sculptures add to the importance and grandeur that Victorians sought in their cemetery monuments. Saint John memorializes a deeply religious German Lutheran, George Ellwanger, and the Weary Pilgrim, with its broad granite base designed by the prominent Rochester architect, Claude Bragdon, recognizes the important status achieved by the wealthy wool merchant, Aaron Erickson.

The Weary Pilgrim rests on top of the Aaron Erickson family monument, Section G, Lot 27. It was sculpted in 1882 by the Italian artist, Nicola Cantalamessa-Papotti.

THE ARCHITECTURE OF MOUNT HOPE MAUSOLEUMS.

When King Mausolus of Caria (now Turkey) died in 353 B.C., his wife Artemisia built a tomb for him that, 140 feet high with 36 columns and topped by a four-horse chariot of marble, became one of the Seven Wonders of the Ancient World.

And although a devastating earthquake somewhere between the 11th and 15th century A.D. destroyed the splendid tomb, Artemisia started something that continues to this day -- the mausoleum.

Probably the most ambitious mausoleum since King Mausolus is the Taj Mahal in India built in 1631. There are also creditable examples of this type of burial structure in Mount Hope Cemetery -- 74 of them, in fact.

To the builders of these Mount Hope mausoleums, burial six feet under was either anathema or an inadequate after-death statement. Whatever the reasons for occupants of these visible tombs to commission them, these mausoleums are today a fascinating study in architectural styles and tastes over the 156-year history of Mount Hope Cemetery.

Egyptian culture must have caught the imagination of General Jacob Gould (1794-1867), because he built his mausoleum in the hillside of Section C in the Egyptian style. Above the entrance is a winged orb, a symbol of the sun god, Re. Here, it is symbolic of the power that can recreate and means, "God, Lord over all, Creator." The mausoleum is topped by an Egyptian obelisk, another sacred symbol of Re.

Nathan Stein (1823-1908), founder of Stein-Bloch Clothes, built the largest mausoleum in Mount Hope Cemetery. It sleeps 20 permanent residents, and there is ample room left over for a lively party.

Here is a mausoleum in the gutsy, unadorned style of the Greek Doric order. The four columns supporting the architrave sit directly on the floor without any pedestal bases; they are tapered with a slightly convex profile. The Greeks discovered that straight lines tend to look as if they sag, whereas gradually curved lines look straight to the naked eye. The Greeks fluted their columns to express the compression implied by the load-bearing function of the columns and also to distinguish the columns from the background masonry.

The Stein mausoleum sleeps 20 and presents the masculine facade of Greek Doric style.

The elegant mausoleum of Alfred Ely in Section D is like a miniature Greek temple. Ely's columns have Ionic capitals, which are a more delicate and ornate convention than the Doric order represented in the Stein mausoleum.

With their curvilinear details, Ionic capitals smack of the organic, recalling leaf and plant forms. Also, the columns themselves are taller and thinner by comparison to the Doric order, and they rest on elegantly molded bases.

Those architectural authorities who seek sexual connotations to things refer to the Doric order as "manly beauty, naked and unadorned," while Ionic is the feminine order.

Alfred Ely (1815-1892) was a U.S. Congressman from Rochester during the Civil War. He had an embarrassing escapade in the early days of the war when in 1861 he packed a picnic lunch and rode his carriage out from Washington, D.C., to witness what he considered to be a frolic that would end in an ignominious retreat for the Confederacy. However, it turned out to be the Battle of Bull Run, a resounding Confederate victory, and unfortunately, Congressman Ely was captured by the Confederates and ended up languishing in a Richmond prison for six months before the Union negotiated his release.

Romans were preoccupied with the curve. What the post-and-lintel was to the Egyptians, and the colonnade to the Greeks, the arch was to the Romans.

Frederick Cook's mausoleum, Section L, displays a Roman arched entrance. The arch rests on squat pilasters, which are column forms that are not freestanding.

When you spin it 180 degrees, the arch becomes a dome. And Cook's mausoleum sports a handsome colonnaded dome.

Frederick Cook (1834-1905) probably deserves such a prominent mausoleum. He owned and operated the famous Cook's Opera House, formerly on the site of the Rochester Convention Center; he was a major investor in the Pullman railroad car, and he was also a commissioner of the cemetery.

The William G. Stuber (1864-1959) mausoleum pays respect to the classic architecture of Greece with two Doric columns framing the entrance. Otherwise, its interplay of simple rectangles belongs to the Modernistic style. Similarly, another handsome 20th-century mausoleum next door adopts Romanesque features with its arched entrance and decorative keystone. Grove Avenue, Section MM.

Lewis Henry Morgan (1818-1881) is considered the father of the science of anthropology. This attribution comes from his seminal studies of the culture of the Seneca Indians.

His mausoleum would be classified as High Victorian Gothic. It is constructed of Medina sandstone, which is living up to its name -- it is turning to sand. The erosion only adds to the spookiness of this shadowy vault in the hillside along Ravine Avenue.

The practically universal feature of Gothic architecture, of course, is the pointed arch -- here seen in the fenestrations at the top of the two steeples. The steep, pointed gables and the elaborately pierced balustrade are also Gothic-inspired.

When we use the term "modernistic," we mean the 1920s, 30s, and 40s. To some young people, these dates may seem antediluvian rather than modern. In architectural styles, however, the Modernistic period was a period of rejection of the elaborate ornamentation of previous styles.

Modernistic ornament is predominantly rectilinear. And rectangles over rectangles define the facade of the Gustav Erbe (1852-1931) mausoleum in Range 5. Even the stone planters in front of the mausoleum have square tops. The Stuber mausoleum pictured on the previous page displays similar Modernistic treatment.

In the Ray Hylan (1906-1983) mausoleum, Range 10, there are rectangles plus two simple circular columns. The facade is all basic geometrical shapes. But the addition of propeller-driven commercial airplanes cut into the stone entablature adds a personal touch and reflects the occupant's pioneering accomplishments in his profession.

At left is the rugged Whitbeck mausoleum, Section I, with massive columns of roughly carved stone. The post-and-lintel construction reflects an Egyptian inspiration. The miniature Greek temples, opposite page, also in Section I, are mausoleums for the Johnston family and are executed in Greek Doric style.

Man's best friend is the one pet that receives memorial recognition in Mount Hope Cemetery. Above, a little girl rests her head on a trusty friend. This stone carving is in Section I.

Carlo, at right, was cast in bronze and decorated the front lawn of the Pratt mausoleum in Section L for more than a century before he was stolen in 1992.

A marble sculpture of a long-haired terrier with a bow around her neck in Section S carries the inscription: "I am her little Flossie watching over her while she sleeps."

One child's grave in the children's burial section of Range 1 is in the form of a bear sculpted in reddish-brown granite.

THE GRAVE
OF
NATHANIEL ROCHESTER
DIED MAY 18 1831
AT 72

OF ADAMS ROCHESTER
CIRCUMSTANCE

We called her

ANNA

—

Previous pages: Col. Nathaniel Rochester (1752-1831), left-hand page, is the founder of the city that bears his name. The Latin inscription, "Si monumentum requiris circumspicie," translates, "If you would seek his monument, look about you," and the winter view from his gravesite in Section R, Lot 11, on top of Rochester Hill is a magnificent panoramic scene of downtown Rochester.

Col. Rochester brought his slaves with him when he moved from Maryland. Although he freed them, some stayed in his employ. On the right-hand page is the headstone of one of Col. Rochester's slaves with its simple, poignant message -- a woman whose complete identity consisted of a first name.

Above is a view of Rochester Hill to which site Col. Rochester's remains were transferred when the Buffalo Street burying ground was vacated to build a city hospital.

At right is the monument for Jonathan Child (1785-1860) on Rochester Hill, Section R, Lot 10. Child was Col. Rochester's son-in-law and the city's first mayor.

JONATHAN CHILD

BORN

IN LYME NEW HAMPSHIRE

JAN. 30, 1785,

DIED

OCT. 27, 1860.

FREDERICK DOUGLASS.

The gravesite of Frederick Douglass in Section T, Lot 26, is located on the lower portion of the slope that leads up to the mount called Hope and beyond it down to the Genesee River. You see Mount Hope when facing west. When you face east from Douglass' gravesite, you look toward Douglass' proud statue in Highland Park Bowl and the site of Douglass' former home at the corner of South Avenue and Robinson Drive. The statue and homesite are three or four city blocks away. It is perhaps a similar distance to the river. In the 1850s the passage between the river and Douglass' home was frequently walked at night by slaves escaping from their bondage in the South.

Frederick Douglass played a significant role in the operation of this Underground Railroad, a system by which runaway slaves traveled principally by boat on navigable portions of the north-south river system. Rochester was a penultimate stop. Here, slaves would be hidden in private residences, many of them in Douglass' South Avenue home, until the next boat transported them the 50 miles across Lake Ontario to Canada.

The escaping slaves had to be hidden even here in New York State where slavery was prohibited, because scouts from the South were constantly on the lookout for blacks, and those who could not produce proof that they were free were shipped back to the South and returned to slavery.

The Underground Railroad operated under severe secrecy. For example, the A. F. Wolcott house at Mount Hope Avenue and Sanford Street, had a tunnel from its basement to the river so that disembarking slaves didn't have to take a surface route to safety in the Wolcott's basement.

Of course, Frederick Douglass was himself an escaped slave being sought by scouts. He was the son of a black slave mother and a white overseer father on a Maryland plantation. His half-white blood did not save him. He was a slave until he ran away, but he finally bought his official freedom from his owner for about $1250.

Frederick Douglass (1818-1895), the runaway slave who fought for the abolition of slavery and published his famous abolitionist newspaper, The North Star, in Rochester, died in Washington, D.C., but chose to be buried in Mount Hope Cemetery because Rochester was the city that had supported him for many years.

JOHN

JOHN SNELL, RAILROAD HERO.

The New York Central train out of Albany via Auburn left the Canandaigua station 10 minutes late on the evening of February 16, 1857. It was headed for Rochester where it was scheduled to arrive at 11 p.m. The train was filled with passengers and mail.

At the throttle of the mighty steam locomotive, the Daniel Webster, was a 37-year-old engineer, John Snell. Emblazoned below the name, Daniel Webster, on the side of the engine was the message: "I still live." This classic, wood-burning engine was the pride and love of young Snell.

Four miles west of Canandaigua, the Daniel Webster approached a curve at 20 m.p.h. when Snell noticed seven bars of track iron that had been maliciously set across the tracks. Snell tried desperately but couldn't stop the train in time. He stayed at his post helpless, and the train jumped the tracks throwing him 20 feet down the embankment into mud and water.

The conductor, the brakemen, the fireman, and the passengers largely escaped serious injury, but Snell lay mortally wounded in the mud. The brakemen lifted him onto their shoulders and carried the wounded engineer to one of the passenger cars that had not derailed. A doctor aboard the train tried to treat Snell, but he died of internal bleeding 15 minutes after the accident . His last words were for his fireman. "Tell him," Snell whispered, "to take care of my engine."

One of the seven bars of iron track was cut into three pieces and another was driven into the earth by the force of the locomotive. Snell's body was taken to his home on Lowell Street in Rochester where he lived with his wife and two children. The outpouring of public grief and anger over the murder was tremendous. Extra cars had to be added to trains coming into Rochester from both east and west to carry the numerous mourners to the funeral.

A huge procession from Brick Church to Mount Hope Cemetery engaged nearly all of the public carriages in the city. In addition, the Eagle, National, American, and Clinton Hotels supplied their large omnibus carriages drawn by large numbers of horses to carry the multitude of mourners one and a half miles to Mount Hope.

On John Snell's marble tombstone there is a carved likeness of the Daniel Webster engine and the following epitaph:

"He came to his death in the discharge of his duty as an engineer on the New York Central railroad by means of an obstruction willfully placed on the track in the night. But heroically keeping his post on his engine, the Daniel Webster, to the last, he generously sacrificed his own life for the preservation of those under his charge. This memorial is erected by his fellow engineers, and others, not only as a monument of their respect for his magnanimity as a man but also as a tribute of their esteem for him as a companion and friend."

THE PROSPECT STATION RAILROAD DISASTER.

Fifteen years after the John Snell incident, another railroad disaster killed a honeymoon couple on Christmas Eve. The tombstone inscription in Range 2, Lot 178, tells the whole poignant story:

"In memory of our dear children, Wilbur F. Rice, aged 28 years, 7 mo's, only son of James & Catherine Rice of Titusville, PA, and S. Coralin Jackson, aged 22 years, 5 mo's, 15 days, only daughter of Morris S. & Julia E. Jackson of Henrietta, NY, who were united in marriage on the 5 day of Dec., 1872, and met death together while returning from their wedding tour at the Prospect Station railroad disaster on Christmas eve, Dec., 24, 1872. Waiting in heaven."

Previous pages: John Snell (1820-1857), heroic engineer on the New York Central r.ailroad, is buried in Range 3, Lot 67. The bas relief sculpture in marble is a likeness of Snell's locomotive, the Daniel Webster.

At right, the new chapel, built in 1912 in Gothic Revival style, was designed by J. Foster Warner.

MR. MYERS.
WAS FIRST INVENTOR
OF A SUCCESSFUL
BALLOT VOTING
MACHINE

ROCHESTER INVENTORS.

In his book, *Notable Men of Rochester*, published in 1902, George Bragdon lists 127 names of inventors and notes that "Rochester furnished a larger number of valuable inventions in proportion to its population than any other city in the world."

Bragdon does not include Dr. Josephus Requa (1833-1910), a Rochester dentist, who invented the machine gun. His invention, an apt one for a dentist we believe, was known as the Requa Rifle, and it was first used in the Civil War. He is buried in Section C, Lot 128.

Bragdon also misses the fact that J. Harry Stedman (1843-1922) invented the fuzzy pipe cleaner, but of course that invention is trivial to all but a dwindling number of pipe smokers. Bragdon does recognize, however, that Stedman invented the streetcar transfer. This simple device, still used on city buses, consists of a small slip of paper that permits a passenger to continue a journey on a different line without paying an additional charge.

Stedman's initial idea proved too elaborate and insulting to many people. He had printed small drawings of various human types, some 20 or so classifications -- man, woman, boy, girl, black, white, Oriental, bearded -- which conductors were supposed to punch out to identify the transfer holder and thereby prevent cheating. When travelers became incensed at the pictures chosen for them by conductors, Stedman devised a simpler approach that has been wisely adopted by today's bus-transfer systems. Stedman is buried in Section MM, Lot 90.

James Goold Cutler (1848-1927) was a Rochester architect who turned inventor when a client asked that a system for central collection of mail be built into a tall office building that he commissioned Cutler to design. Cutler's solution was the Cutler mail chute, still used everywhere today.

Cutler's idea was so good that it had many imitators. In one U.S. Post Office case an important letter was lost and in the course of a lawsuit, the letter was found stuck in one of those mail-chute imitations. The judge ruled that in the future the U.S. Post Office would only pick up mail from Cutler mail chutes because of their dependability, so Cutler got a monopoly on the mail chute business, a highly desirable situation financially. As a consequence, Cutler is entombed in a fancy, expensive mausoleum in Section MM, Lot 91, proving in a sense that he could take some of it with him.

HIRAM SIBLEY.

Hiram Sibley (1807-1888), all-American entrepreneur, became the richest man in 19th-century Rochester. His wealth remained unsurpassed until George Eastman's great success. Sibley conceived the idea of building a transcontinental telegraph line. When he proposed his scheme to other small telegraph company owners in New York State, they ridiculed his plan to connect the Atlantic and Pacific by telegraph communication. Their assembled wisdom went as follows: It would be next to impossible to build such a line. If built, it would surely be destroyed by Indians in the territories. Or if not destroyed by Indians, certainly by nature in mountain blizzards and avalanches. Lastly, it would not be profitable.

Sibley, not persuaded, said it would be built even if he had to do it alone. His grand conception became Western Union.

Sibley then considered connecting North America to Europe by way of Alaska and Siberia. He was magnificently entertained, as well as encouraged financially, at the royal court of Czar Alexander, and Western Union constructed a telegraph line along the coast to Alaska and had built 1500 miles in Siberia when Cyrus W. Field announced the successful laying of the Atlantic cable.

Although Sibley abandoned the Siberia project, he persuaded Czar Alexander to sell Alaska to the U.S. and became the person most singularly responsible for the acquisition of our 49th state.

Previous pages: Jacob Myers (1841-1920), left-hand page, is buried in Range 4, Lot 68. He invented the first voting machine which was used in Lockport, New York, in 1892. Rochester used Myers' voting machines in all districts in 1896.

Seth Green (1817-1888), right-hand page, is buried in Section S. He invented the fish hatchery and gained national fame when he hatched 15 million shad and quadrupled the fish population of the Connecticut River.

At right, the Hiram Sibley family monument, Section D, Lot 143, is followed in ascending order by three imposing obelisks. Classic symbols were Victorian favorites, and the obelisk, borrowed from the ancient Egyptians, was particularly impressive. Initially, the obelisk was a symbol for the sun god, Re. To Victorians it symbolized a belief in God as creator and lord over all.

SUSAN B. ANTHONY.

"The right of citizens of the United States to vote shall not be denied or abridged by the United States or by any State on account of sex."

So reads the Nineteenth Amendment to the United States Constitution. The words were written by Susan B. Anthony, the pioneer crusader for the rights of women. She composed the wording at her home, today a national landmark, at 17 Madison Street, Rochester. But it was 14 years after she died that these 28 words became law. Some highlights along the way include:

• February 15, 1820. Susan B. Anthony is born in Adams, Massachusetts.

• 1852. National convention of women is a joint planning effort of Susan B. Anthony and Elizabeth Cady Stanton.

• 1868-1870. Anthony and Stanton publish a liberal weekly called *The Revolution.*

• 1869. The National Women's Suffrage Association, headed by Anthony and Stanton, supports action through a constitutional amendment.

• 1872. Susan B. tests voting-rights laws in Rochester, New York. She leads a group of women to the polls in that year's presidential election. As the ringleader, she is arrested, tried, convicted, and fined. "May it please your honor," she said, "I will never pay a dollar of your unjust penalty."

• 1878. "Anthony Amendment" granting women's suffrage is introduced in Congress by Senator Aaron A. Sargent of California. Reintroduced annually, it is either kept off the floor or defeated until 1919.

• 1881-1900. Susan B. compiles a four-volume *History of Women's Suffrage.*

• 1888. Susan B. organizes the International Council of Women, involving 64 nations.

• 1892-1900. Susan B. is president of a merger of two women's-rights groups that become the National American Women's Rights Association.

• March 9, 1906. Susan B. Anthony dies at 17 Madison Street in Rochester.

• 1918. House of Representatives passes 19th Amendment, 274 for, 136 against.

• 1919. Senate passes 19th Amendment, 66 for, 30 against.

• 1920. 19th Amendment ratified by the states.

Susan B. Anthony (1820-1906) is buried in Section C, Lot 93, which is marked by this modest marble headstone. She lies next to her sister, Mary, and other members of the Daniel Anthony family.

BORN ON THIS SITE.

A few hundred feet south of the old gatehouse in Mount Hope Cemetery and quite near Mount Hope Avenue is a modest, flat stone with a simple but arresting inscription:

NANCY HARRIS
QUACKENBUSH
1818 - 1900
BORN ON THIS SITE

Born in the cemetery? Well, not exactly. But the story is interesting nonetheless.

Mount Hope Cemetery opened in 1838, the land having been purchased in 1836. So, Nancy Harris' birth preceded the cemetery by two decades.

When Nancy was born in 1818, a log cabin stood on the site of her present grave. The cabin was built by her maternal grandfather, Jacob Miller. Miller came here prospecting for land in about 1808. He started farming land in the Elmwood/Mount Hope Avenue area. The western part of his farm formed what became the southeast portion of the old section of the cemetery. In 1810, Jacob Miller built a one-room log cabin on that portion of his land.

They had to barricade the door of the cabin at night to keep out bears and wolves. When the British invaded Charlotte in the War of 1812, Miller feared he might lose his highly valuable team of oxen to the American cause. He had been told to surrender them. So, Miller's son, Harvey, drove the oxen through the woods into a marsh (now Sylvan Waters in the cemetery) and hid there in the thick brush with the oxen for several days until the all-clear signal came.

When Jacob Miller and his family moved out of the house in 1816, he let his daughter and son-in-law, Amanda and Daniel Harris, have the cabin. It was a crowded little cabin, because Amanda and Daniel arrived from Otsego County with nine children in tow. And Nancy hadn't even been born yet.

When Nancy Harris was born in 1818, the area surrounding her home was still wild. George G. Sill -- traveling from Old Lyme, Connecticut, to Rochesterville to open the village's first bookstore -- happened on the area at night, and Nancy's father had to escort him through the area because the road was so blind, and there were so many wildcats, bears, and wolves in the neighborhood.

Here is where little Nancy spent her early years. She saw the forests cut down and roads made from trails, the hills lowered and marshes filled. Around her the city grew so rapidly that it became the country's first boomtown.

Nancy married a boatbuilder, John Quackenbush, on December 18, 1845, and settled in the town of Greece. In the 1850s, Nancy and John, along with their young daughter, Mary, and Nancy's mother, Amanda, lived at 7 Marshall Street in Wadsworth Square while John supported them with his boatbuilding trade, a highly needed craft in the days of the Erie Canal. Unfortunately, John Quackenbush died in the late 1850s, so Nancy's marriage was all too brief.

Widow Nancy spent her final years in Buffalo, where she died of influenza at the age of 82. She was buried on April 3, 1900, in Mount Hope Cemetery on the site of her birth where the log cabin had disappeared perhaps more than 60 years before.

MAY FIELDING, WHITE SLAVE GIRL.

In the Home for the Friendless plot in Section P, there is a modest tombstone with the following intriguing inscription:

C.A.M.
The white slave girl
known as May Fielding
died June 2, 1857, aged 15.
I was a stranger here
and ye took me in.

MARIA SCOTT, COLORED.

In the Daniel Harris plot in Section C, there is another headstone that begs a story. The stone reads:

IN MEMORY OF
MARIA SCOTT COLORED
WHO DIED
JUNE 8, 1842
AGED 18 YEARS & 19 DAYS

Nancy Harris Quackenbush (1818-1900), with the arresting inscription on her tombstone, is buried in Section H, Lot 21.

NANCY HARRIS
QUACKENBUSH
1818 — 1900
BORN ON THIS SITE

THE TOMBSTONES OF ARCHITECT CLAUDE BRAGDON.

Claude Bragdon (1866-1946) designed so many distinctive residences and other buildings in Rochester that he is regarded principally as an architect. But his enormous talents were remarkably diverse. The title of his autobiography, More Lives Than One, appropriately alludes to his work as an architect, a Broadway stage-set designer, writer, Brahmin priest, and expert in the occult. He designed arches, bridges, floats, light shows, book covers, posters, stained glass, bookplates, furniture, and countless other decorative objects. Not the least of his design efforts was cemetery monuments. Mount Hope is graced by a number of Bragdon's creative monument designs. Here are several of the more prominent ones:

• James G. Averell, Section D, Lot 143.

• Emily Sibley Watson / James Sibley Watson, Section D, Lot 141.

• William R. Seward, Section F, Lot 31.

• Antoinette Pumpelly Perkins, Erickson / Perkins, Section G, Lot 27.

• Henry A. Ward / Alice Mabel Ward, Section G, Lot 76.

• William E. Werner, Section MM, Lot 116.

In most of these plots, Bragdon designed the large family monuments as well as individual headstones. An interesting feature of many Bragdon monument designs is the incorporation of a reincarnation motif. Bragdon himself was a firm believer in reincarnation. In 1925, he wrote in his book, *Old Lamps for New*, "Although the doctrine of reincarnation appears to be not susceptible to proof, as a belief it is natural and reasonable. It is in full accord with science which recognizes neither creation nor destruction, but only endless transformation. Moreover, it clears up many of the mysteries and contradictions of life, casting a new light on the problem of human misery and seeming injustice, something which the single-life theory utterly fails to do."

A symbol for reincarnation is the endless knot, and this motif finds its way into several Bragdon monument designs.

At right, the William Rossiter Seward monument, Section F, Lot 31, reflects the Art Deco style of architect Claude Bragdon.

A detail view at left shows a woman holding an eternal flame.

VICTORIAN SYMBOLISM IN MOUNT HOPE.

Victorians abandoned the skull and crossbones and other death-as-a-grim-reaper symbols of their forefathers in favor of more romantic motifs. The willow-tree-and-urn motif, which was introduced in the late 1700s, led the change to these romantic symbols. The skull became a cherub. The words "graveyard" and "burial ground" were replaced by "cemetery" which means a sleeping chamber -- in this case a kind of dormitory where the dead await resurrection.

The principal reason for this change in attitude toward death was an awakening to a more optimistic outlook on it. The stern notion that all sin would be punished was replaced by a belief that sin could be forgiven and good deeds and righteousness would be rewarded.

Some of the symbols to be found in Mount Hope Cemetery and their meanings are listed below:

ANCHOR: hope.

ANGEL: messenger between God and man.

BROKEN COLUMN: end of life, sorrow.

CHRISMA: a crosslike shape formed by a combination of two Greek letters, chi (X) and rho (P) corresponding to CH and R of the word, Christ, hence a symbol for Jesus Christ.

CROSS: salvation.

CROWN: righteousness, victory, triumph, glory, resurrection.

CROWN ON A CROSS: sovereignty of the Lord.

DAISY: innocence, gentleness, purity of thought, youth.

DAFFODIL: desire, beauty, deep regard.

DOGWOOD: Christianity, divine sacrifice, triumph of eternal life, resurrection.

DRAPERY OVER ANYTHING: sorrow, mourning.

EAGLE: symbol for Saint John.

FLAME: eternity.

GRAPES AND LEAVES: Christian faith.

HAND: symbol of leaving.

IHS: abbreviation of Latin phrase, Jesus the savior of men.

INVERTED TORCH: extinction of life.

IVY: friendship, faithfulness, undying affection, eternal life.

LAMB: innocence, meekness, most common child's marker.

LAUREL: special achievement, distinction, success, triumph.

LILY: purity, innocence, resurrection.

LILY OF THE VALLEY: purity, humility, renewed happiness.

MORNING GLORY: brevity of life, farewell, departure, mortality.

OAK: stability, strength, endurance.

OBELISK: an upright four-sided pillar, gradually tapering as it rises and cut off at the top in the form of a pyramid, symbol for the Egyptian god, Re, who held the power to recreate.

POPPY: eternal sleep, consolation.

ROSE: unfailing love, beauty, hope.

SCALLOP SHELL: symbol of the Crusades, pilgrim, pilgrim's journey, resurrection.

SHEAF OF WHEAT: God's harvest.

STELE: Greek small column or pillar terminating in a cresting ornament and used as a monument.

TREE TRUNK: cut-off life.

URN: Greek symbol of mourning.

WINGED GLOBE: a symbol of the Egyptian sun god, Re; on Victorian monuments it is symbolic of the power that can recreate and, with the wings, means, "God, Lord over all, creator."

WREATH: memory.

Variations of the endless-knot motif appear on the four surfaces of the James Sibley Watson Celtic cross, Section D, Lot 141. Architect Claude Bragdon used the endless knot in his monument designs to symbolize a belief in reincarnation.

THE LANTERN FACTORY FIRE.

Rochester has had several devastating fires, but none was more catastrophic in loss of human life than the Steam Gauge and Lantern Works fire on the evening of November 9, 1888. Just before 7:30 p.m., a fire started in the basement of the lantern factory situated between the Genesee River and Center Street at the Upper Falls (the Court Street falls).

The night watchman noticed the fire as it reached the first floor and ran to give the alarm. In his panic he neglected to warn 60 men and boys who were still working on the 5th, 6th, and 7th floors of the factory.

When the firemen arrived, the flames were shooting up the elevator shaft cutting off that escape route and the lower floors were completely consumed by the fire. The boiler in the basement exploded and flames leaped out of broken windows on every floor. The trapped workers screamed for help.

Firemen managed to place extension ladders against the building and rescued 10 men before the walls of the building started to collapse.

An enormous crowd of thousands of onlookers gathered around the burning building and severely hampered the efforts of the firemen. The firemen stretched nets for the trapped workers to jump into, but the workers couldn't see them in the engulfing smoke. Many jumped anyway, in desperation. One man plunged to his death landing in the Genesee River; another man was killed when he landed in a pile of scrap tin.

Every fire unit in the city was on the scene. They now fought to keep the fire from spreading to the Williams and Hoyt shoe factory next door. Other nearby factories provided holding rooms where doctors who had rushed to the scene gave emergency treatment to the few who had escaped alive. Horse-drawn ambulances, police and delivery wagons, taxis and private carriages carried the burned victims to St. Mary's Hospital and City Hospital.

It took days to uncover the bodies from the debris of the totally destroyed building. In the end, 38 men and boys perished. For days afterward, funerals wound through the streets of Rochester to Mount Hope Cemetery. Six bodies were so badly burned that they could not be identified. A special community funeral was staged for them in the Washington Rink, the largest public accommodation in the city. Over 2000 people attended. A procession of more than 40 carriages took officials and mourners to Mount Hope Cemetery where the burials were made near the Firemen's plot in Section BB. A large stone monument stands there today with a bronze plaque inscribed with the details of the fire.

The magnitude of the disaster affected the community deeply. One policeman took in a young widow with a six-month-old baby. Among the dead was Alonzo Stone, whose wife had been killed a year earlier. His death left their preschool daughter an orphan.

The cause of the fire, even after weeks of investigation, was never determined.

PENMAN AND PRINTER.

In flowing, graceful lines engraved into hard granite, the tombstone of Clara T. Dennie, Section AA, Lot 74 -- in calligraphically more elaborate lettering than the following -- reads:

Clara T. Dennie, Penman
1912-1984
Teacher of Beauty
Lover of Beauty
Lover of Life

On the north bank of the deepest kettle in Mount Hope Cemetery, Section G, Lot 152, is the monument of Reuben Manley. He was a printer and each line of the inscription on his stone is rendered in a different typeface. The following gives the idea but does not replicate the 1842 typefaces:

THE
Typographical Profession.
REUBEN MANLEY,
Printer,
DIED,
DECEMBER 22nd, 1842,
AGED 24 YEARS.
RESQUIESCAT IN PACE.
ROCHESTER, N.Y.   DEC. 24, 1842.

Previous pages: Overlooking Section U, future home of the author, with Glen Avenue on the left.

At right, the 55-foot Firemen's monument in Section BB. In the left foreground, a marble fireman's helmet rests on one of the headstones.

THE GRISLY TALE OF BOYD AND PARKER.

When the settlers in America rebelled against British rule in 1776 and waged a war for independence, many Indians remained either neutral or friendly to the Americans. However, others chose to side with the British. For example, the Seneca Nation, which occupied Genesee Country and was the largest of the Six Nations of the Iroquois League, made a treaty in 1764 binding their allegiance to the British, and they did not annul that treaty when war broke out.

Some American settlers, especially recent arrivals from Great Britain, also remained loyal to the crown. Finally, the British established their great stronghold of the interior at Fort Niagara. During the war the combination of Indians, American loyalists, and British wreaked havoc and destruction on the western fringe of American settlements in the Mohawk, Hudson, and Susquehanna valleys.

Joseph Brant, the English name of a Mohawk Indian, became the leader of the Indian forces. His brother-in-law, an Irish landowner in the Mohawk Valley and loyal to Great Britain, had sent Brant to England for an education.

John Butler, an American loyal to England and who was Deputy Superintendent of British Indian Affairs before the war, became Lieutenant Colonel of what was known and feared as Butler's Rangers.

Both Brant and Butler were notorious for the ferocity of their raids on American settlements. From a safe haven in Genesee Country and with British support, Brant and Butler led their troops over Indian trails for as far as 300 miles to destroy American farms and villages. To induce the Indians to take the warpath, the British offered rewards for Yankee scalps and prisoners delivered to Fort Niagara.

Matters got so bad that Congress finally ordered the destruction of the hostile tribes. In 1779, General George Washington ordered General John Sullivan to invade the territory of the Six Nations. Proceeding through the Susquehanna and Chemung river valleys, his army of 5000 men destroyed Indian towns, orchards, and crops and reached the head of Conesus Lake on the evening of September 12, 1779. They camped there before their planned attack on the principal Seneca Indian town, known as Genesee Castle, from where the head of the Senecas, Chief Little Beard, ruled his Indian nation.

There was a disagreement among Sullivan's men over the precise location of the great Seneca village, the maps indicating it was on the east side of the Genesee River and Sullivan's Indian guides insisting it was on the west side. To settle the matter, General Sullivan ordered 23-year-old Lieutenant Thomas Boyd to take four riflemen and an Indian guide and during the night locate the town and the best route to it.

Lieutenant Boyd was very bright with a promising army career. Boyd served under Major Parr, who said of him, "He was of fine physique, engaging manners, brave almost to recklessness. He was endowed with the qualities which would command attention." Parr's only reservation about young Boyd was a matter of maturity. Parr felt that the strapping youth did not yet demonstrate "the cool judgment or firmness which would fit him for a leader."

Instead of five men, young Boyd took 28 and headed west. By daylight, he reached a point where he thought the map indicated that the village ought to be. But he found the area deserted and decided to return to the army encampment. What he didn't realize was that he had stumbled on a small Seneca village that had been vacated in anticipation of Sullivan's advance and that, yes indeed, the Senecas had, since the map was made, moved their great village of 128 large and elegant houses surrounded by thousands of peach and apple trees and hundreds of acres of cultivated fields to the west side of the river near the present village of Cuylerville. It was truly the granary of the western allies of King George III.

Of course, an army of 5000 men does not march through the wilderness unnoticed. Brant's forces and Butler's Rangers descended on Genesee Castle to defend the great village and to defeat Sullivan's forces, if possible. They planned an ambush, the historic Groveland Ambuscade.

And of course, they mistook Boyd's returning scouting party for the advance of Sullivan's army and lured them into their ambush. Boyd's men fought bravely, but 18 of them were massacred by the overwhelming forces of Brant and Butler.

Lieutenant Thomas Boyd and Sergeant Michael Parker, however, were captured and taken to Genesee Castle. There they met Joseph Brant, Lieutenant

Alexander Millener (1762-1865), Range 2, Lot 231, who lived 103 years, was General George Washington's drummer and led American troops into countless battles against British forces. His drum is part of the collection of the Rochester chapter of the Daughters of the American Revolution.

Colonel John Butler, and Chief Little Beard. Boyd, who was a Freemason, knew that Brant had become a Mason while he was going to school in England, and now, Boyd transmitted the secret signs of brotherhood to Brant and appealed for protection. Brant, honoring his Masonic vows, promised to provide it, but then he was called out of the village on other business.

This left Boyd and Parker to Colonel Butler and Chief Little Beard. Butler questioned Boyd relentlessly about Sullivan's army -- its size, its position, its intentions, its destination -- all apparently to no avail. From some reports, Boyd refused to answer. However, later, Butler wrote to headquarters giving all of the wanted details concerning General Sullivan's campaign. Butler also said that he found Boyd to be particularly intelligent and well informed. In any case, when he was through with the questioning, Butler turned Boyd and Parker over to the Indians. It was left to Chief Little Beard to devise what happened next. Before him was an officer and a soldier of the army that was laying his country to waste.

Most historians dismiss the torture with a sentence:

Irene A. Beale: "Little Beard then directed acts of unspeakable cruelty."

1877 History of Monroe County: "Boyd was put to the most inhuman torture."

Semi-Centennial History of the City of Rochester: "So terrible was the torture that the recollection of his sufferings was vivid for more than 60 years, aroused the keenest anguish, and could not be related without shuddering."

George H. Harris: "The most frightful tortures that savage natures could invent were inflicted on these unfortunate men."

Simon L. Adler: "Boyd's body was terribly mutilated, and he had been subjected to the most exquisite tortures."

Mary Cheney Elwood: "They were then subjected to a series of the most inhuman and revolting tortures, the bare recital of which causes the bravest heart to quail and the bravest cheek to blanch."

Jenny Marsh Parker: "...horribly tortured and killed, their headless remains found."

That night, September 13, 1779, Lieutenant Boyd and Sergeant Parker were led to a large oak tree, today called the Torture Tree. Around them fires blazed lighting up the night that was soon to become dawn.

Boyd and Parker were stripped naked before the assembled crowd and brutally whipped until their backs were badly welted and bruised. The fiendish series of tortures by the Indians were devised to keep the victims alive and conscious for as long as possible. It was as if the Indians viewed every aspect of the two naked bodies before them and determined a torture for each part.

After the beating, they meticulously pulled each and every nail from Boyd's and Parker's fingers and toes. They cut off the right ears, their noses, and their tongues. They plucked their right eyes from the sockets and left them hanging down their faces. They cut Boyd's and Parker's genitals so that they hung from strands of flesh a foot below their normal position.

Then the Indians cut open the abdomens of Boyd and Parker, pulled out the upper ends of their intestines, severed them from the stomach and fastened the ends to the tree trunk. The Indians then drove Boyd and Parker around the tree unravelling their intestines. The iridescent membrane wrapped around the tree until their intestines were wholly drawn out.

They ripped open their chests and withdrew the beating hearts. Boyd's heart was found fastened to his right hand. The two men were finally beheaded.

In the bright, morning light at the end of the night-long torture, one Seneca Indian took the head of Lieutenant Boyd, impaled it upon his spear and led a dance around the Torture Tree and the mutilated bodies of the two Americans. The Indians then fled their village at the imminent approach of Sullivan's army.

The first men from Sullivan's army to discover the scene on September 14 were Captain Elnathan Perry and Private Sanburn.

Lieutenant Boyd's partially skinned head had been placed on a log, its terror-stricken left eye staring blankly at the scene before the Torture Tree and its gaping mouth in a silent scream. Sergeant Parker's head was missing and was never found.

General Sullivan, after describing the tortures in his journal report said that the details should not be mentioned out of decency, but the grisly account of Boyd and Parker soon filled the newspapers throughout the country.

Sullivan's soldiers buried Lieutenant Boyd and Sergeant Parker beside a clump of wild plum trees at the junction of two small creeks, about 50 feet from the Torture Tree.

General Sullivan, appalled at the savagery of the Indians, ordered the complete destruction of the village of Genesee Castle and the miles of orchards,

waving corn, and every vegetable that could be imagined.

The white Indian woman, Mary Jemison, said when the Indians returned to take possession of the village, "We found that there was not a mouthful of sustenance left, not even enough to keep a child one day from perishing from hunger. And our corn was so good that year."

After Genesee Castle, Sullivan's army gave up the march and returned home. The Indians, their economy ruined, fled to Fort Niagara to seek protection and subsistence from the British.

But the travails of Boyd and Parker were far from being over. Events were such as not to allow them a peaceful rest beneath the wild plum trees.

In 1807, robbers violated the graves to take clothing as sacred relics. In 1830, other curiosity seekers again rummaged among the bones and found, among other bits and pieces, four metallic buttons that were used on U.S. Army uniforms at the time of the Revolutionary War, thereby authenticating the burials.

Then, in 1841, 62 years after the ghastly torture, Professor Samuel Treat, principal of Temple Hill Academy in Geneseo, gave a July Fourth speech saying it was shameful that no monument honored the fallen soldiers. Rochester newspapers took up the cause, and soon there was a movement to exhume the remains and transfer them to the newly established and prestigious Mount Hope Cemetery.

A site in Section R, Lot 85, to be called Patriot Hill, was selected and a temporary wooden monument, painted to resemble marble, was erected for the very grand ceremonies that were planned.

On the afternoon of August 19, a flotilla of six canal boats with five military companies aboard -- the Williams Light Infantry, the Union Grays, the City Cadets, the Rochester Artillery, and the German Grenadiers -- along with invited guests and a horde of journalists glided south on the Genesee Valley Canal to a cheering crowd all along the canal route.

In Cuylerville the next day, there were parades and lavish meals. The bones, buttons, and bits of cloth of Boyd and Parker were placed in a specially designed wooden urn. Similarly, the bones of Boyd's men who had been massacred and buried near Groveland were placed in a large wooden box that everyone called "the sarcophagus."

Even the descendants of the grave robbers of 1807 and 1830 gave up their relics of buttons and bits of uniform and patriotically placed them with the appropriate bones.

At Colonel Cuyler's house, under a grove of stately oaks, a platform and seats were set up. Survivors of Sullivan's army -- Major Moses Van Campen, 85, Captain Elnathan Perry, 81, and Mr. Sanburn, 79 -- sat on the platform with a group of distinguished speakers, which included Professor Samuel Treat and the mayor of Rochester.

Henry O'Reilly, the Rochester newspaper publisher offered a resolution: "That the streams at whose juncture was buried the mangled bodies of Boyd and Parker, one of which streams has hitherto been nameless, and the other named after the savage chief whose ferocity was signalized by the shocking tortures of the gallant Boyd, shall hereafter be named in honor of those fallen soldiers -- the latter Boyd's Creek, and the former Parker's Creek; that those streams, and the mound at their juncture, may commemorate the names and services of those martyrs through all time, while grass grows and water runs."

As the sun set, the flotilla with its recently exhumed cargo slowly glided north arriving in Rochester at sunrise. One local poet described the procession to Mount Hope Cemetery:
"With drooping flag and muffled drum,
And slow and measured tread,
Behold, on their proud march they come,
The bearers of the dead."

If the Cuylerville ceremonies were impressive, Rochester outdid itself. Here were Governor William H. Seward, the Adjutant General, the Surgeon General, two Major Generals, two Brigadier Generals, five Colonels, four Majors, the Mayor and Aldermen, three Reverend Messrs., five military companies, Revolutionary War officers and soldiers, the event committee of inordinate size and distinction, a hearse, pallbearers, the urn, and the sarcophagus. Church bells rang and a marching band played. And thousands of citizens watched.

The patriotism lasted through the day. The very next morning, people were arguing, bickering, and accusing. One political party, the Democrats, accused another, the Whigs, of depositing bears' bones on Patriot Hill, even though they had witnessed the careful exhumation in Cuylerville. Newspapers kept the controversy raging for years.

Meanwhile, in Mount Hope Cemetery, the wooden urn and sarcophagus sat on the ground for 23 years next to the temporary marbleized wooden monument

and gradually deteriorated from heat and rain and winter's blasts.

Finally, one day in 1864, a cemetery employee went up to Patriot Hill, scraped up some bones lying on the surface of the ground, and buried them in potter's field, Section Y. Patriot Hill was made more level so that more plots could be laid out and sold. The ground that was so grandly dedicated in 1841 to Revolutionary War patriots was sold as separate plots for somewhere between $2000 and $3000.

The story of Boyd and Parker has its most poignant ending at this point, but there is a contemporary postscript. The grand ceremony accompanying the transfer of the remains of Boyd and Parker to Mount Hope Cemetery occurred 62 years after their deaths. In 1903, after another 62 years had passed, the Irondequoit chapter of the Daughters of the American Revolution found the soldiers' remains in potter's field and reburied them once again in a plot marked by a boulder with a bronze plaque in Section BB, Lot 123, where they lie today and will, it is hoped, rest in peace for more than another 124 years.

BUFFALO BILL, JOHNNY BAKER, & THE WILD WEST SHOW.

In 1872, Henry A. Ward, geologist and University of Rochester professor, went on a buffalo hunt in Nebraska. His guide was William F. Cody who later became world famous as Buffalo Bill. Ward was quite impressed with young Cody and encouraged him to move to Rochester. Cody later took the advice and wrote Ward that he and his family were "hitting the trail for Rochester."

The Cody family lived in Rochester from 1873 to 1877 and returned from time to time thereafter. It was here that Buffalo Bill developed his combination traveling circus, theatrical troupe, and stunt show known as the Wild West Show. His first attempt -- a melodrama called Life on the Border -- played to packed houses at Rochester's Corinthian Hall. In the show Cody displayed his abilities as an expert horseman and superb marksman, while his children and their friends played the parts of native American Indians.

Unfortunately, in 1876 his only son, Kit Carson Cody, died of scarlet fever at the age of 5 years. That year, seven-year-old Johnny Baker became the son that Buffalo Bill lost. Cody made Johnny a world-champion rifle shot and Wild West Show star. Johnny's parents didn't seem to mind that their son was away most of the time, but they rejected Buffalo Bill's attempts to adopt the boy.

In May, 1883, Buffalo Bill launched the first version of what became his famous Wild West Show. He brought the show to Rochester one month later, in June. It was staged at the huge Driving Park track, and 5000 Rochesterians saw the first performance. There were 60 Indians, a herd of buffaloes, a gang of cowboys, Texas steers, and sharpshooting Johnny Baker. It was, as the newspaper said, "a complete panorama of wild western life."

However elated Buffalo Bill was at the fantastic success of the Wild West Show, he was also devastated in that year of 1883 by the death of his daughter, Orra Maude. She was buried next to Kit Carson in Mount Hope.

Buffalo Bill's show and Johnny Baker not only wowed them in Rochester. Most of Europe's royalty saw the show. Archduke Francis Ferdinand of Austria so admired the special rifle Baker used that Johnny gave it to the Archduke as a gift. King Edward of England saw the show in London in 1905 and was so impressed that he wanted to congratulate the protagonists personally. Boy wonder Johnny Baker gave the king a hearty western-style handshake, creating a storm of comment in the newspapers over this breach of protocol. King Edward himself seemed charmed.

Buffalo Bill's second daughter, Arta, died in 1904, the year before the King Edward incident, and she was buried next to Kit and Orra. Buffalo Bill himself died in 1917, and despite attempts to bring his remains to Mount Hope Cemetery, the state of Colorado retained his burial at Lookout Mountain, Colorado. However, Johnny Baker died in 1931 and is buried in Section I, Lot 149.

Kit Carson Cody (1870-1876), five-year-old son of Buffalo Bill Cody, is buried in Range 2, Lot 215, next to his sisters, Orra Maude, who died in 1883, and Arta Cody Thorp, who lived long enough to marry (1866-1904).

DAVID BARTON'S ROLE IN FLOUR MILLING.

Flour milling in Rochester had been going on for more than a decade at a relatively brisk pace before the Erie Canal opened in 1823. Then production exploded with the resulting easy, inexpensive access to markets in the east and Europe.

A decade later, in 1833, there were four mill races in town and 18 mills equipped with 78 run of stones. Rochester shipped 300,000 barrels of flour annually, which was one-third of all the flour going down the Hudson River. Rochester's preeminence in the flour business was solidly established.

Just two years later, Henry O'Reilly wrote in his newspaper, the Rochester Daily Advertiser: "There are now within the City of Rochester 21 mills, with 108 run of stones, capable of manufacturing 5000 barrels per day."

Such capacity consumed an immense amount of wheat. Now, not only the rich Genesee Valley furnished raw material, but so did land around Lakes Erie and Ontario, Ohio, and even Canada.

In 1901, Rochester's output was a million and a half barrels. That was the zenith in production for the Flour City. Now it was the Midwest's turn.

The early mills were models of advanced industrialization and automation. In the Hervey Ely mill, for example, grain from the rich farmlands throughout Genesee country was carried up mechanically in buckets to the top of the five-story mill. From there, the grain descended through successive stages of cleaning, grinding, cooling, sifting, and packing until the final product rolled out in sealed barrels onto the decks of canal boats aimed for eastern U.S. markets or transfer to ships sailing for Europe. The whole manufacturing operation was accomplished without the grain ever once being touched by the miller's hand.

Rochester flour was world-famous for its quality. Of course, there were various types, grades, and brands, including graham flour which was invented here by Sylvester Graham. But the best was truly superior. It was highly acclaimed at the Crystal Palace Exposition in 1851 in London. Queen Victoria herself expressed a preference for Rochester flour. It made especially good cakes, she maintained.

In 1844, Queen Victoria ordered 6000 barrels of Rochester flour for the royal kitchens. A lot of cakes, that.

Production of 300,000 barrels of flour annually created another substantial industry: barrel making. And to make that manufacturing process efficient required special tools to plane the wooden barrel staves. So, still another industry developed in Rochester to fulfill the need for barrel staves: tool making. It was David Barton who led and excelled at the business of making machine tools.

Barton's machine-tool factory was located on Brown's Race but on the west side of the raceway, away from the gorge and the waterwheels that provided the necessary machine power. This did not deter Barton. He arranged to buy power from a waterwheel that ran a mill across the raceway from his factory. He then transferred that power across Brown's Race through an ingenious system of gears and shafts running overhead to his building. There, he further divided the power vertically so that each floor of his multi-story operation was supplied with the mechanical power to operate all of his metal lathes and other machinery.

Rochester is still a center for the machine-tool industry in America, and David Barton played a significant role in creating it.

David R. Barton (1805-1875) designed and manufactured tools to make flour barrels and other products made of wood. He is buried in Section H, Lot 13, beside his family monument, a handsome obelisk.

Above, the monument to publisher Frank E. Gannett (1876-1957), Section MM, Lot 247, incorporates an endless-knot motif designed by the famous landscape architect, Fletcher Steele (1885-1971). He selected granite and obsidian (volcanic glass) for the monument materials.

At right is the cast-iron Florentine fountain located in the north entrance. It was originally installed in 1875 and completely restored in 1985. A female figure holds a container from which water springs and drops into an upper basin, then spills into a second basin, and from eight lions' mouths the water finally falls into a reflecting pool.

MONUMENT MATERIALS.

Almost everywhere you look in Mount Hope Cemetery there are monuments. And they are particularly noticeable because of their verticality. They rise out of the hills, the valleys, and the flat areas to create a mighty chorus of the dead in a collective hope of eternal life. In one sense, the stones themselves achieve the hope, because in their search for permanence, the Victorians selected the best monument materials.

Their New England forefathers made tombstones of marble and slate, but the Victorians preferred granite. It was particularly hard and durable. And it could be obtained in a wide variety of colors and crystalline textures to suit individual tastes.

Marble was an important second choice. Here again, marble comes in a variety of grades, some of which are proving to be quite permanent, some not. Many of the figure sculptures are executed in marble.

There are few slate monuments to be found in Mount Hope. The Victorians noted that the slate monuments of their New England ancestors tended to flake thereby destroying their carved inscriptions. However, one monument designer who preferred and selected slate for his own monument and for the stones of members of his family was Fletcher Steele. Steele chose black slate of exceptionally high quality and created a set of four colonial tablets (Section C, Lot 215), with details taken directly from early New England stones.

An interesting monument material with many examples in Mount Hope is molded metal. The metal is almost 100 percent zinc and as it ages, the zinc forms a tough and durable oxide that protects the metal underneath from deterioration. The zinc oxide is bluish gray in color and to the casual observer has the appearance of stone. Molded-metal monuments were quite inexpensive and could be ordered from catalogs that listed countless forms, shapes, symbols, sculptural elements, etc. Custom pieces could be molded with personal messages. These were then sandwiched together and fastened with bolts to create attractive and interesting three-dimensional monuments. Surprisingly, these relatively inexpensive monuments are proving to be quite permanent. Century-old, molded-metal markers in Mount Hope Cemetery show no discernible loss of detail.

"TIS AN OLD SAW, CHILDREN SPEAKE TRUE."

So said the 16th-century English poet, John Lyly. Children still express their thoughts openly. The experienced tour guides from the Friends of Mount Hope Cemetery give tours to nearly 1000 school children annually. Afterward, the children sometimes write down their impressions. Here is a sampling from some fourth graders on one of the author's tours.

"I enjoyed the cemetery. I really liked the trees. I liked the fountain. The statues were neat. I liked it so much I want to take my mom," said David.

"This field trip was the most informing in my lifetime," said young Kevin, "I would love to be buried in Mount Hope Cemetery. I bet you would too."

"I liked the tour so much I want to bring my family," said Amy.

Some of these young people have a feeling for the historical aspects of the cemetery. For example, history is what particularly struck Alex. He said, "I especially liked the way you explained what Susan B. Anthony, Frederick Douglass, and George Selden did when they were living."

Robert was also historically impressed. He wrote, "I liked the part when we went up the hill and saw the builder of the Erie Canal." (Myron Holley, Section G, Lot 159.)

What catches the eyes of other children is the great variety of design features that man has placed in the cemetery over the last 156 years. Referring to the rock fountain in Sylvan Waters, Mark said, "I liked the part about the pond. It looked like it had a big beehive in the middle. It was a super trip."

Commenting on the prevalent motif for reincarnation, Rachel said, "The endless knot was cool."

And Paul picked a rock to like. However it was no ordinary rock; it was the boulder flecked with jasper that the great geologist, Henry A. Ward, found in Georgian Bay, Ontario. Paul said, "The best thing I liked was the dotted rock."

Some young people even have a taste for the macabre. Joel said, "I liked the big house they burned the bodies in."

Previous pages: An infrared scene at the top of the highest hill in Section G.

At right, in Section C, is a molded-metal marker, "Our Willie, over in the summer land."

Above, Mount Hope was a primeval forest before it became a cemetery. The glacial hills and valleys were judiciously cleared of trees to make room for human burials, yet much of the forest remains.

At right, the first burial to be made in Mount Hope Cemetery was that of William Carter (1773-1838), Section A, Lot 4. He died August 17, 1838, and his burial occurred before the cemetery was dedicated on October 3, 1838. Transfers from older, abandoned burial grounds account for the many earlier death dates found in Mount Hope.

WHAT KILLED OUR FOREFATHERS?

Benjamin Campbell came to Rochester in 1820 as a general merchant, but the profits to be made in flour milling were so attractive that he entered the business and by 1835 was successful enough to build an elegant Greek Revival house that today is a house museum of the Landmark Society of Western New York. Unfortunately, just a few years after his impressive house was built, Campbell went bankrupt when the price of flour plummeted. His house was sold at public auction in 1841.

Frederick Whittlesey, a prominent businessman and judge, bought the house in 1852, and the Whittlesey family lived there well into the 20th century.

The Campbells and the Whittleseys are buried in Mount Hope Cemetery -- the Campbell family occupying Lots 56 and 56 1/2 in Section G, and the Whittleseys, Lots 79 and 79 1/2, Section G.

Let's take them as typical middle-class families in boomtown Rochester of the 1800s and list the family members in chronological order of their deaths, their age at death, and the official cause of death from the Mount Hope interment index. First, the Campbells:

• George Campbell, 1838, aged 1 year, summer complaint.
• Julia Campbell, 1840, aged 9 years, scarlet fever.
• Azel Ensworth, 1854, aged 94 years, old age.
• Rufus Meach, 1861, aged 67 years, rheumatism.
• George W. Ensworth, 1865, aged 56 years, paralysis.
• Sophronia E. Campbell, 1882, aged 81 years, old age.
• Benjamin Campbell, 1883, aged 92 years, old age.
• Eliza Jerome, 1888, aged 81 years, nephritis.
• Frances C. M. Hubbell, 1901, aged 74 years, apoplexy.
• John Campbell Hubbell, Jr., 1919, aged 24 years, epilepsy.
• John C. Hubbell, 1922, aged 68 years, arteriosclerosis.
• Francis E. Hubbell, 1938, aged 73 years, apoplexy.
• Martha Hubbell, 1942, aged 71 years, generalized arteriosclerosis.

And the Whittleseys:

• Frederick Whittlesey, 1851, aged 52 years, typhus fever.

• Julia A. Whittlesey, 1866, aged 31 years, convulsions.
• Anna H. Whittlesey, 1890, aged 88 years, senility.
• Thurlow W. Whittlesey, 1892, aged 56 years, apoplexy.
• Frederick A. Whittlesey, 1905, aged 77 years, grippe and pneumonia.
• Mary M. Whittlesey, 1910, aged 78 years, bronchitis.
• William Seward Whittlesey, 1917, aged 76 years, lobar pneumonia.
• Frances C. Whittlesey, 1924, aged 86 years, cerebral hemorrhage.
• Clara J. Whittlesey, 1929, aged 81 years, myocarditis.
• William C. Whittlesey, 1938, aged 69 years, coronary thrombosis.

Today's medical descriptions may be more precise than summer complaint, old age, and senility. And we may call apoplexy a stroke, and grippe, influenza.

Summer complaint was food poisoning that caused severe diarrhea. Without refrigeration, it was difficult to keep food fresh. In colder months, nature provided refrigeration, but not in summer and hence the name of the disease.

The Campbell and Whittlesey families were spared cholera. There were major epidemics of cholera in 1832, 1849, and 1866. The 1832 cholera epidemic killed about 120 Rochesterians and became the principal impetus for establishing Mount Hope Cemetery.

The Campbells and Whittleseys were also lucky in losing only two children, one to summer complaint, another to scarlet fever. In the 19th century, scarlet fever and diphtheria were particularly deadly to children. The most cursory exploration of Mount Hope Cemetery attests to the incredible death rate among children. Rochester was probably not far behind New York City in a typical mid-century year, 1853, when 49 percent of those who died in New York City were children under five.

Victorians who survived childhood tended to live reasonably full lives as can be seen by the Campbells and Whittleseys.

The Yaky family plot, Section E, at right, is enclosed by a cast-iron fence, a detail of which appears above. Many of the family plots in Mount Hope used to have such decorative iron fencing around them, but practical measures of cemetery maintenance caused the sale of much of this fencing in the 1960s and 1970s.

Those Victorians who commissioned monuments of more complexity than the common colonial tablet often chose tombstones incorporating a variety of architectural features. Above, Ionic columns hold up miniature porticoes above which a classical roof has a dentiled cornice. The whole resembles a building, but there is no entrance; it is solid stone. In the Minoan culture of ancient Crete, these were little houses for the soul.

Henry S. Potter's impressive family monument, Section V, Lot 9, at right, includes a stone, bas relief profile of the old man himself (1798-1884). The figures on top represent Hope consoling Sorrow. Potter was the first president of the Western Union Telegraph Company, which was founded by Hiram Sibley.

HENRY S. POTTER,
BORN FEB. 14, 1793,
DIED JAN. 9, 1884.

HARRIET BENEDICT
WIFE OF
HENRY S. POTTER,
BORN SEPT. 13, 1805,
DIED JULY 3, 1881.

POTTER

Previous pages: At left is a seated female figure in marble representing Sorrow. At right and also seated, but carved in granite, is a sorrowful male angel.

Above, stone and vegetation in verdant Mount Hope provide a photogenic juxtaposition. Lilies of the valley grow at left while trees work hard to dominate stone.

At right is the prevalent way of presenting an identifying name on Mount Hope tombstones -- with an appropriate period after it.

A TRAGIC CIVIL WAR ROMANCE.

In 1863, St. Mary's Hospital in Rochester signed a contract with the federal government to provide medical care for soldiers wounded in the Civil War. From 1863 to the end of the war in 1865, St. Mary's became a military base treating over 3,000 wounded soldiers. The hospital received from the government $5.50 per week for each patient.

St. Mary's was founded in 1857 by Sister Hieronymo O'Brien of the Sisters of Charity order. It was this order that arrived on the battlefield in Gettysburg, Pennsylvania, three days after the carnage to alleviate the chaos there. Sister Hieronymo was the first Sister Superior and remained so for the duration of the Civil War.

One of her devoted nurses was Margaret Augusta Peterson, the youngest daughter of Jesse Peterson, 24 Caledonia Avenue, near Spring Street. Margaret was 23, tall and beautiful with black hair and dark eyes. As a nurse at St. Mary's, Margaret changed the dressings and cared for the hospitalized soldiers. She also wrote their letters for them, and when time permitted, she read to them. Margaret devoted her whole time to the wounded soldiers and Sister Hieronymo was particularly grateful to her for her dedication.

Also at St. Mary's at the time was a young medical intern, Harvey Polley Foote, who was similarly 23 years old, tall, dark, and handsome. Harvey arrived in Rochester in December, 1863, after being mustered out of military service as an acting hospital steward. The Rochester Directory listed him as a medical student boarding at 11 Gibbs Street. Margaret and Harvey fell in love, and they soon became engaged to be married.

Smallpox was quite prevalent in those days, and as a preventive measure, it was considered wise for the hospital staff to be vaccinated. Margaret's vaccination was performed by her lover, Harvey. But the vaccine, unbeknown to Harvey, was contaminated. It caused an infection, which developed into gangrene, and on September 1, 1864, Margaret died.

Her death was devastating to young Harvey. He soon fell ill himself and died of typhoid fever at St. Mary's Hospital a month later, October 8, 1864.

Margaret and Harvey are buried side by side with military gravestones at each grave in Section E, just behind the old gatehouse.

CAPTURED IN THE CRATER AT PETERSBURG.

In the summer of 1864, Union forces devised an ingenious plan to blow up the Confederate fort at Petersburg by tunneling beneath it. Four tons of explosives blasted a crater 60 by 170 feet and 30 feet deep. One whole Confederate regiment and an artillery battery were buried. West Pointer E. G. Marshall led the Union assault after the explosion. But the backup to his brave assault was mismanaged or, rather, hardly managed at all because one of those in charge, General James H. Ledlie, stayed behind drinking rum. Marshall and his troops were trapped by the Confederates, who managed to regroup, and were forced to find refuge in the crater. It proved to be no shelter and Marshall was captured. The Confederate officer who captured him took his hat, coat, and valuables. Marshall asked to be taken to General Lee, who immediately recognized the great enemy commander and soundly scolded the officer who had robbed him. Marshall later received a high brevet commission, but the battle at the crater was a Union fiasco.

Previous pages: The Civil War plot, Section BB, contains many of the Rochester soldiers who died in that bloody war. However, more Civil War casualties are buried throughout Mount Hope Cemetery. Rochester contributed 5000 men to the Union cause; two of them became Medal of Honor winners: Warren Carman captured the Confederate flag and a passel of prisoners; Dr. Richard Curran treated the wounded in a hail of bullets.

At right, the family monument of Bvt. Major General Elisha Gaylord Marshall (1829-1883), Section G, Lot 193, is surmounted by a carved marble sheaf of wheat symbolizing God's harvest. To date, the gravestones of 8 Civil War generals of the Union Army and 5 generals of the New York State Militia, who fought in the Civil War, have been located in Mount Hope Cemetery.

Following pages: At left is the poignant Civil War monument, 22 feet high, depicting the company bugle boy and a weary soldier carrying the Union flag. The bronze sculpture is the work of Sally James Farnham, a noted American sculptor who studied under Frederick Remington. A bronze plaque on the base of the statue is inscribed:
> *"By fame's eternal camping ground*
> *Their silent tents are spread*
> *And glory guards with solemn round*
> *The bivouac of the dead."*

At right is the headstone of Charles D. Howell (Section W, Lot 9), 108 Regiment, New York State Volunteers, who fell wounded at the storming of Fredericksburg, December 13, 1862, and died in the 5th Division Hospital, Falmouth, December 22, aged 18 years, 1 month, and 22 days.

CHARLES D. HOWELL,

108 REGIMENT N.Y.S. VOL'S

WHO FELL WOUNDED AT THE

STORMING OF FREDERICKSBURG,

DEC. 13, 1962,

AND DIED IN THE 5 DIVISION

HOSPITAL FALMOUTH DEC. 22.

AGED 18 YEARS, 1 MO. & 22 DAYS.

A SOCIOLOGY CLASS LOOKS AT MOUNT HOPE.

Each spring and fall for a number of years, the author has taken a Pittsford Sutherland High School sociology class on a tour of Mount Hope Cemetery. Here are a couple of reports that resulted from one of the tours.

"Before this field trip, I thought the cemetery was another boring place which no one goes to see. As it turned out this trip was interesting. I never thought that a gravesite could show a lot about a person: name, age when he passed away, sex, how wealthy he was by the size of his tombstone, and in some cases, his race. We saw a grave which implied that this man was black because he was a slave. I especially liked the scenic points of the cemetery. There were historical points that our guide told us about. The glacier thing was very interesting."

Another student wrote:

"My favorite field trip was the excursion to Mount Hope Cemetery. I found the symbols on the gravestones very interesting. The stone in the form of a tree was fascinating. It symbolized the cut-off life as a stump of a cut-down tree. On the stump there were other sawed-off branches which symbolized the lives of the person's relatives who had died before. And also the ivy which was carved around the stone tree trunk symbolized everlasting love. Other symbols were a cloth draped over an urn, a weeping willow, a cherub, and the never-ending knot. This symbolized the never-ending cycle of life. I also enjoyed learning about the famous people buried in Mount Hope. For example, the man who really invented the automobile but had his idea stolen from him by Henry Ford. Also Susan B. Anthony who fought for women's rights and Margaret Woodbury Strong and how she founded the Strong Museum with her collections. Lastly, Frederick Douglass and how he escaped slavery to fight for emancipation and civil rights through his speeches and newspaper."

At right, the 54-foot-high Dr. Hartwell Carver monument, Range 2, Lot 104. Carver (1789-1875) is credited with initiating and developing the idea of the transcontinental railroad. He saw his dream come true and helped to drive the final golden spike that connected the Atlantic and Pacific oceans by rail.

At left is the 10-foot Italian marble figure atop the Carver monument. She represents Hope.

Previous pages: The cut tree trunk was a favorite Victorian tombstone symbol for a cut-off life. The Carter monument at left is executed in granite. At right is another tree-trunk gravestone. When little Laura Knapp died, a group of her friends who were stone carvers collaborated on this complex, intricate monument. Above the granite base carved to resemble a pile of rocks is a single piece of marble that includes the basic tree trunk with a basket of flowers. Multiple symbols appear on the tree trunk: lily of the valley = purity, lily = innocence, ivy = undying affection, morning glory = brevity of life.

Above, carved ivy twines around a stone cross. The cross represents Christian salvation and the ivy stands for friendship, faithfulness, undying affection, and eternal life.

At right, a cherub (a servant of God) leans on an overturned torch to snuff out the torch flame, thus symbolizing the end of a human life.

CEMETERY SUICIDE.

John J. Gorres grew up in a prominent Savannah, Georgia, family of French ancestry. His father was a leading citizen in Savannah and financially very successful. John married, raised a family, and seemed quite settled until his wife died when he was in his late forties. Her death disturbed him enormously, to the extent that he decided to leave Savannah and start a new life with his children elsewhere.

He chose Rochester, New York. John opened a piano and music store on State Street in the early 1880s and for a few years business was excellent. He was often seen about town riding in his handsome one-horse cabriolet. He and his children established a comfortable home at 27 Elizabeth Street.

But depression haunted Gorres. Shortly after moving to Rochester, his youngest son, still a boy, died, adding deeply to his despondency. He was left now with one other son and a daughter.

John Gorres was a devout Christian and began to spend an extraordinary amount of time in religious study. His business declined to the extent that he finally closed his large State Street store and began to sell pianos with help from his son out of their Elizabeth Street house. His children and friends noticed that John often talked to himself, frequently in a strange agitated manner.

On Tuesday, September 7, 1886, John Gorres -- now a man in his early fifties with two wonderful children, a fine house and an adequate business, a substantial bank account in Flour City National Bank, and significant property holdings in Savannah -- entered the Wheeler & Wilson pawnshop downtown and purchased not one but two revolvers. The guns were nearly new -- one a 32-caliber, ivory-handled revolver of the Blue Jacket style and the other a 32-caliber Smith & Wesson.

On Wednesday evening he went to his bedroom, but instead of undressing for bed, he changed his clothes. He put on black trousers, light-colored socks, low shoes, and an old alpaca coat. On his head he wore a silk hat. Gorres sat down at a table in his bedroom and wrote a letter addressed "To my children" and signed "Your father." The letter said that his heavenly father had called him away, as he was God's son, and that he would return in a few days to take them to heaven with him. He loaded his two guns and wrapped them in brown paper and newspaper. Then he left his house and started walking to Mount Hope Cemetery.

Gorres crossed the Clarissa Street bridge (now Ford Street bridge) and instead of proceeding down Mount Hope Avenue toward the main cemetery entrance, he turned sharply right and followed the road along the feeder canal (now Wilson Boulevard). This brought him to the west boundary of the cemetery. He climbed the hill to a portion of Section M where in those days hedges were planted to define the boundaries of the family plots.

He sat down with his back resting on one of the hedges and his legs stretched out in front of him. He unwrapped his guns, cocked them, and held the ivory-handled revolver in his left hand and the Smith & Wesson in his right -- one pressed against his left temple about an inch from his left eye and the other similarly pressed against his right temple. He squeezed both triggers. The left gun fired killing John Gorres before the right gun fired. He was determined not to fail in this suicide.

At 4:30 on Friday afternoon, two cemetery gravediggers, Ferdinand Barl and Henry Hohmann, their work done for the day, were leaving their tools behind a hedge in Section M when they noticed two legs stretched out from the other side of the hedge. There was John J. Gorres, seated upright with a bullet hole in his left temple, blood stains down his face, neck, and onto his shirt collar and shirt front. His left hand grasped an ivory-handled revolver. One chamber of the gun was empty. Another revolver had apparently dropped from his right hand and fallen between his knees. It was cocked and fully loaded. A piece of brown paper and some newspaper lay just beyond the body.

Previous pages: At left, a child with head raised toward heaven and hands folded in prayer is carved in marble. This statue was stolen in 1992. At right, a hand reaches out from under a drapery. The hand is a symbol of leaving, and the drapery represents sorrow and mourning.

At right, the deepest kettle in Mount Hope Cemetery is in Section G. These deep conical depressions were formed by glaciers 12,000 to 14,000 years ago.

Following pages: An old stone road leads from the north entrance of Mount Hope up to Indian Trail Avenue.

HENRY

He is not dead, this child of our affection,
But gone unto that school,
Where he no longer needs our poor protection,
And Christ himself doth rule.

SAMUEL WARD,
SON OF
SAMUEL L. & SUSAN W.
SELDEN,
BORN
SEPTEMBER 4, 1847,
DIED
NOVEMBER 4, 1848.

Previous pages: At left, in Section G, the sculpture is a likeness of Henry Lee Selden, son of Samuel Lee and Susan Ward Selden, born March 18, 1846, died June 25, 1858.

At right, a marble girl angel.

Above, day lilies, thoughtfully planted many decades ago, bloom every spring by father August's and mother Wilhelmina's gravesite.

At right, the tombstone of Mary, with a period, is shaded by plant growth in verdant Mount Hope Cemetery.

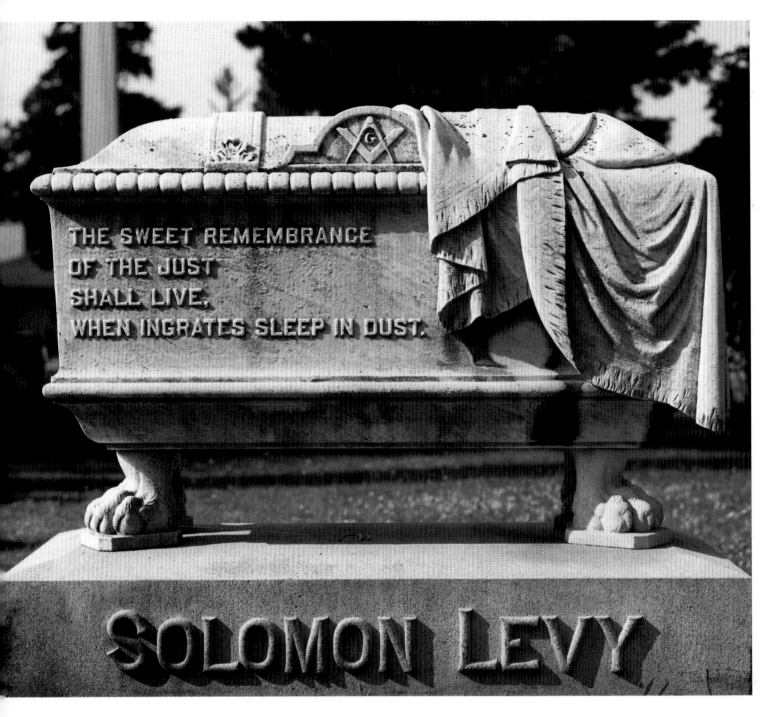

THE SWEET REMEMBRANCE
OF THE JUST
SHALL LIVE,
WHEN INGRATES SLEEP IN DUST.

SOLOMON LEVY

Previous pages: Glen Avenue cuts through the cemetery landscape between Cedar Avenue and Grove Avenue.

Above, Solomon Levy's unusual monument in Range 5 begs the question, "Who were these ingrates?"

At right, the Van Hoesen granite monument in Section MM depicts a stylized, early 20th-century angel holding a wreath, which symbolizes memory.

Previous pages: Water fills one of the four glacial kettles in the cemetery, which is called Sylvan Waters. Water was an important cemetery feature to Victorians; it is a symbolic representation of a cleansing spirit.

Above, the many thousands of trees in Mount Hope remind us that the area was a forest before it became a cemetery. Trees were very judiciously removed to make room for gravesites and yet retain the parklike setting desired by Victorians.

At right, in Section D, a female figure kneels before a cross, the Rock of Ages, which meant salvation for 19th-century Christians.

A CASE OF CANNIBALISM.

The 1800s were a period of exploration to the far-off reaches of our planet. In 1881, the United States Army launched such an expedition of discovery to the Arctic.

The exploratory party consisted of 25 men headed by Lieutenant Adolphus W. Greely. The second in command was a 35-year-old army officer from Rochester, New York, Lieutenant Frederick F. Kislingbury. They sailed from a Newfoundland port to establish a colony for scientific study in arctic ice on the north shore of Lady Franklin Bay.

In the course of their expedition, the group reached 83 degrees and 24 minutes -- farther north than any previous explorers. They made gravity measurements nearer to the North Pole than before; they ascertained the climatic conditions of Grinnell Land; they determined the first magnetic variations in that region, and they made glaciological studies and tidal observations. From a scientific viewpoint, the expedition was a great success. From a human standpoint, it was quite different.

The expedition party was left with a year's supply of food. More supplies were planned for each summer of the three-year expedition, because summer was the only possible season for supply ships to reach a camp that far north. But through gross army bungling and the sinking of one supply ship, those supplies didn't reach the stranded team.

Lieutenant Kislingbury became a principal hunter for food because he was such an accurate marksman. In 1884, when the food stock was desperately low, he shot a rarely seen polar bear only to watch the killed bear float out of reach on an ice floe.

In January, 1884, when the available food supply was down to a few pounds of meat and bread per man, Greely called the men together and divided the food equally. But Private Charles B. Henry began to steal food. Finally, Greely called a meeting of the men to act on Henry's thefts. The desperate men, with one voice, condemned Henry to die and he was shot.

The men, reduced to living on sealskins from earlier hunts, migrated south in search of food supplies that might have been dropped off at various designated alternative points. But there was no food. Kislingbury, now 38, died of starvation on June 1, 1884. The expedition's surgeon, Dr. Octave Pavey died on June 6, committing suicide in the last stages of starvation. By the time rescue finally came three weeks after Kislingbury's death, 18 of the 25 men had

died. Lieutenant Greely and six other survivors were found on Cape Sabine on June 23, 1884. None of them had eaten one particle of food for 48 hours.

The dead, at least those whose bodies could be found, were wrapped in cotton, tied with hemp, put in metal caskets with 52 bolts on the lid and marked with a warning not to open.

There was ample reason for the warning. When Kislingbury's casket arrived in Rochester, it was buried in Range 3, Lot 177. Then, rumors began to spread that cannibalism had occurred on the ill-fated expedition. The survivors denied it but there were calls for an examination of Kislingbury's body.

Finally, Lieutenant Kislingbury was dug up from his peaceful rest in Mount Hope Cemetery. The casket was taken to the old chapel; the 52 bolts on the lid were removed, and beneath the Tiffany sconces and chandeliers of the elegant chapel, three doctors -- Charles Buckley, F. A. Mandeville and James Buckley -- performed the examination.

The body of young Kislingbury revealed that an incision had been made from the clavicle downward below the ribs. The skin had been carefully cut away from the flesh and folded back. The flesh was then removed from the ribs and the skin was meticulously laid back over the bones. The back and thighs were treated in the same manner with the skin replaced over the clean bones. The legs were stripped to the ankle joints and the arms to the wrists. Only the hands, feet, and head were not mutilated.

Dr. Charles Buckley said, "Gentlemen, the dissection of this body was the work of an expert. There was no hacking with knives, but it was the work of a sharp scalpel in the hands of a clever anatomist."

Later, Dr. Mandeville made a microscopic examination of the contents of Kislingbury's intestines, which included "striped muscular tissue, epidermis, red blood corpuscles, and oil globules" exactly matching human flesh.

As each of the men died, they had been stripped of their clothes and their flesh had been methodically removed by the expedition's surgeon, Dr. Pavey. Those men who died after Pavey had their bodies more brutally mutilated to feed the living.

At right, vandalism in Mount Hope is a serious problem. But also, settling and shifting of the earth over the last century and a half have toppled some stones. The cause of a lost arm on this sculpture is not certain.

GEORGE BALDWIN SELDEN

BORN SEPT. 14, 1846

DIED JAN. 17, 1922

INVENTOR OF THE

GASOLINE AUTOMOBILE.

Previous pages: A major landscaping project was undertaken on the tenth anniversary of the cemetery in 1848. The trees planted then are now a century and a half old.

Above, this tombstone, Section C, Lot 108, depicts a likeness of the first gasoline automobile, which was invented by George B. Selden (1846-1922) despite Detroit's claims to the contrary. Selden held the patent, but Henry Ford did not believe in the U.S. patent system and used Selden's idea. Selden sued and an eleven-year court battle ensued. Ford paid royalties to Selden but kept on making cars.

At right in Section G, Lot 76, is the tombstone of Henry A. Ward (1834-1906), geologist. The boulder was found by Ward in Georgian Bay, Canada. It is flecked with the semi-precious stone, jasper.

HENRY A. WARD

ELIZABETH D. WARD
1828 —

BORN
183

DIED
190

HENRY MEIGS
1802 —

WHERE IS GEORGE EASTMAN BURIED?

Perhaps the most frequent question asked by tourgoers in Mount Hope Cemetery is: "Where is George Eastman buried?" It is a reasonable question for no other individual in Rochester's history did more to help this city realize its claims to excellence than George Eastman. He is fondly and gratefully remembered by Rochester's residents. And it is natural for them to want to pay him tribute by visiting his gravesite.

The great success of his company, the Eastman Kodak Company, made Eastman enormously wealthy. But he spent relatively little of that wealth on himself and much of it on his community and its institutions -- a considerable number of which he himself founded.

But George Eastman, arguably the city's most prominent citizen, is not buried in prestigious Mount Hope Cemetery, although there was a connection between his burial and Mount Hope.

In the last months of his life, Eastman suffered from a painful disease involving the hardening of the cells in his lower spinal chord. It was a progressive disease that increasingly robbed him of his physical and mental capacities.

George Eastman died at 12:50 p.m. on March 14, 1932, at the age of 77 years. He wrote a note: "To my friends -- My work is done. Why wait?" And then he shot himself.

Lewis B. Jones, manager of Kodak advertising and longtime Eastman associate, said, "George Eastman played the game to the last. By his own hand, he lived his life, and by his own hand, he ended it. To those who knew the orderly working of his mind, his passion for being useful, always useful, his dread of an illness that made him mentally as well as physically inactive, his act can be understood. A great man. At the end of the chapter he wrote his own 'finis.'"

Eastman's body was taken to Mount Hope Cemetery where it was cremated. His request to be cremated was as far as he took his death arrangements. He did not, as most other prominent Rochester citizens did, buy a plot in Mount Hope Cemetery and supervise the design and erection of a monument.

Since Eastman had no other family, a few of his friends and associates at first suggested that his remains might be buried in Waterville, New York, his birthplace and where his mother was buried. But more thoughtful minds suggested a special memorial area at the entrance to Kodak Park at 1669 Lake Avenue.

The memorial was dedicated on September 15, 1934. Eastman's brilliant head of research, Dr. C. E. Kenneth Mees read the dedication. There, beneath a giant, cylindrical stone of pink and gray Georgia marble lie the ashes of George Eastman. One side of the stone has a bas relief sculpture of a woman holding an eternal flame, the other side, a sculpted man representing science and industry. The stepped, circular depression of the memorial park is surrounded by weeping beeches, and at lunchtime on warm sunny days the steps are filled with Kodak workers sitting eating their lunches or chatting.

OLDEST MOUNT HOPE RESIDENTS.

James Hard took up permanent residence in Mount Hope Cemetery at the age of 111 years. It is believed that he is the oldest man to be buried in Mount Hope. Hard was born in Victor, New York, in July, 1841. He died in March, 1953, at the age of 111 years, 9 months. Hard was a veteran of the Civil War, serving from 1861 to 1865, and for years after he was a distinguished -- some might say, professional -- participant in local parades. At the age of 101 he was the honorary chairman of the 1943 Rochester Lilac Festival. He is buried in Range 1, Lot 168.

Cynthia Fitzpatrick, however, was believed to be 118 when she was buried in Single Grave 15, Row 387, Range 3. She was born of slave parents in Mississippi on Christmas Day, 1864, during the presidency of Abraham Lincoln. And she died in Rochester, after having lived here since 1955, on February 22, 1983. Her advanced age was verified by a thorough search of school records and recollections by herself and others.

These ages may seem hard to beat, but there are many challengers in the wings in Rochester today.

At right, with a third of a million burials in Mount Hope Cemetery, there are an equivalent number of stories to tell. On these pages, we've touched on just a few.

Following pages: The valley below was once a swamp that was elaborately drained in the latter half of the 19th century by tunneling 500 feet through a high ridge. The result was the considerable expansion of Section L, which today has many mausoleums and significant family monuments.

INDEX

ACKNOWLEDGMENTS

We are particularly indebted to The Friends of Mount Hope Cemetery for their encouragement and support. Several trustees also assisted us directly in the preparation of this book's content. Jack McKinney, especially, made extraordinary contributions that were invaluable and varied. With his incredible knowledge of the cemetery, he contributed generously to the text and photographic content. He provided constant encouragement to both of us and also proved to be an enormously useful researcher, grammarian, and proofreader. Elizabeth Schmidt was a superlative researcher for several stories and provided valuable input for the overall text. Richard Brown and Shirley Stephens supplied essential Civil War and other data. Stephen Thomas, director emeritus of the Rochester Museum and Science Center, has been an inspiration on the subject of Mount Hope Cemetery for many years with his vast knowledge and fascinating Mount Hope tales. Marilyn, the photographer's wife, with her highly developed artist's taste and judgment, was an indispensable critic and helper in the photographic content of the book. Josef Johns elevated the design of the book to optimal possibilities and, as a very experienced reader, enhanced the appropriateness of the text. We are also very thankful for the significant help of Leon Creek in handling book orders.

Frank A. Gillespie
Richard O. Reisem